CRAZY QUILTING in a Weekend

25 home decor
projects that you
can make in
no time

Flora Roberts

CREATIVE HOMEOWNER®, Upper Saddle River, New Jersey

First published in the US in 2005 by

CRE**A**TIVE
ARTS & CRAFTS

An imprint of Creative Homeowner®,
Upper Saddle River, NJ

Creative Homeowner® is a registered trademark of
Federal Marketing Corporation

First published in 2005 by Cico Books Ltd
32 Great Sutton Street, London EC1V 0NB
Copyright © Cico Books 2005

Text copyright and project designs copyright © Flora Roberts

Current printing (last digit) 10 9 8 7 6 5 4 3 2 1

Crazy Quilting in a Weekend

Library of Congress card number: 2004113740
ISBN 1-58011-241-2

Illustrations by Anthony Duke
Edited by Sarah Hoggett
Photography by Gloria Nicol
Designed by Christine Wood
Styling by Julie Hailey

The publishers would like to thank The Dulwich Trader,
9–11 Croxted Road, London SE21 8SZ for the kind use of jewelry

CREATIVE HOMEOWNER
A Division of Federal Marketing Corp.
24 Park Way
Upper Saddle River, NJ 07458

www.creativehomeowner.com

Printed and bound in China

contents

living-room style 4
Box Pillow 6
Armchair Throw 12
Circular Pillow 16
Silk Fan Pillow 20
Lampshade 24

kitchen pieces 28
Fruit Bowl Cover with Beaded Edging 30
Placemats and Coasters 34
Tablecloth 38
Chair Cover 42
Tabletop Basket 46

in the bedroom 50
Cosmetics Case 52
Jewelry Box 56
Laundry Bag 60
Blanket with Crazy Patchwork Border 64
Bolster 68
Quilt Tied with Rosettes 72
Dressing-table Runner 76
Pillowcase 80
Scented Sachet 84

gifts and heirlooms 88
Handbag 90
Folder 94
Velvet Bear 98
Beach Bag 102
Sun Hat 106
Star Decorations 110

techniques 114

templates 122

index 128

conversion chart 128

❯ box pillow ❯ armchair throw ❯ circular pillow ❯ silk fan pillow ❯ lampshade

living-room style

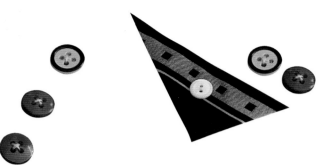

box pillow

The green striped fabric and olive green brocade that I selected for this pillow belong to the same color group, but they needed another color to bring them to life. A shocking pink velvet ribbon saved the day. Colored buttons add to the "craziness" of the design, but also emphasize the shape of the patchwork star.

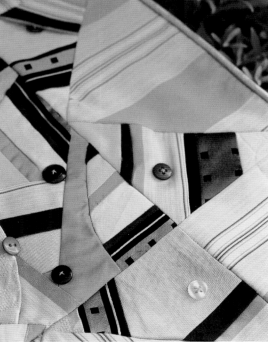

The finished pillow measures 16 x 16 x 4 in. ½-in. seam allowances are included throughout.

YOU WILL NEED

- ❱ Tracing paper and pencil
- ❱ Cardstock or template plastic
- ❱ ½ yd. muslin for foundation fabric
- ❱ ¾ yd. striped silk
- ❱ Strips and scraps of silk and brocade
- ❱ 1¾ yd. 2-in.-wide velvet ribbon
- ❱ Buttons in various colors
- ❱ Two 65-in. lengths of fabric-covered piping cord
- ❱ 20-in. zipper
- ❱ Pillow form or foam cut to 16 x 16 x 4 in.

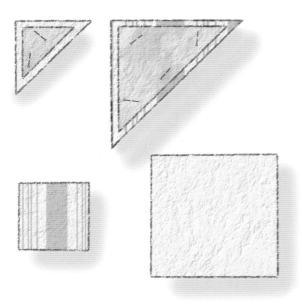

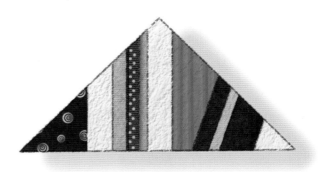

1 Trace the patterns on page 123 onto cardstock or template plastic and cut templates. Using template B, cut eight triangles from the foundation fabric, adding ½ in. all around for the seam allowance. Using template A, cut four triangles from the striped silk, adding ½ in. all around for the seam allowance. Cut four 5-in. squares from the striped silk and a 9-in. square from the foundation fabric.

2 Using strips of silk and brocade, and interspersing pieces of pink velvet ribbon between some of the seams, cover the eight small foundation-fabric triangles with crazy patchwork. (See pages 114–116.)

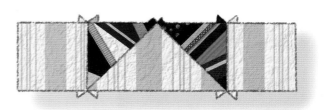

5 With right sides together, machine-stitch the long edges of two crazy patchwork triangles to the short edges of a large striped triangle, to make a rectangle. Repeat with the other triangles. Press the seams open.

6 With right sides together, machine-stitch a striped silk square to each short side of two of the pieced rectangles.

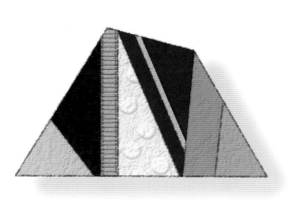

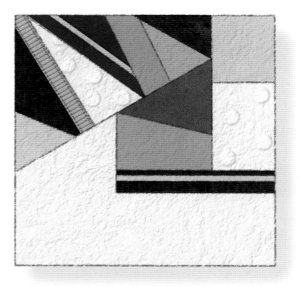

3 Cut irregular-shaped pieces of foundation fabric in different sizes, with sides no less than 4 in. in length. Cover them with strips of silk and brocade, as in Step 2.

4 Machine-appliqué the irregularly shaped crazy patchwork pieces from Step 3 to the 9-in. square of foundation fabric. (See page 116.)

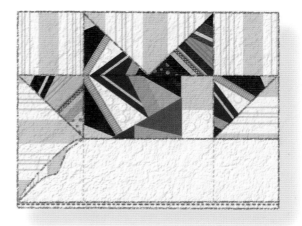

7 With right sides together, machine-stitch the remaining pieced rectangles to opposite sides of the patchwork square, with the apex of the large striped triangles pointing inward, using the illustration as a guide.

8 With right sides together, machine-stitch the three strips together to make a large square, with the apex of each large striped triangle pointing in toward the central square.

9 Press the seams open and the piece flat. Hand-stitch colored buttons randomly to the center and around the edges of the star motif.

10 Pin a length of piping around the edges of the right side of the pillow, with the raw edges facing outward and aligning with the raw edges of the pillow. Gently curve the piping around the corners, cutting small notches in the piping seam allowances on the curves. Machine-stitch in place, stitching close to the cord.

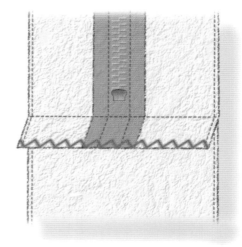

13 With right sides together, baste and then machine-stitch the side section to the top of the pillow, aligning the long raw edges and making sure the seams at either end of the long central section are level with the corners of the pillow top. Cut notches into the seam allowance at each corner, allowing for the curve.

14 With right sides together, machine-stitch the short raw end of the side panel to the short raw end of the zipper section. Zigzag-stitch the raw edges of the seam together and press away from the zipper.

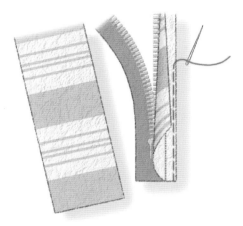

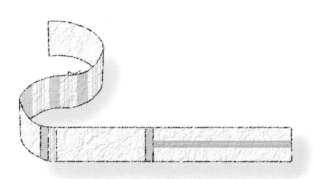

11 To make the zipper section, cut a 6 x 21-in. piece of striped silk with the stripes running parallel to the short edge. Cut the fabric in half lengthwise. Open the zipper and baste one side of it face down to one long edge of one striped piece. Following the instructions on page 121, insert an invisible zipper.

12 For the sides of the pillow, cut two 5 x 15-in. rectangles and one 5 x 17-in. rectangle from the striped silk, with the stripes running parallel to the short edge of the pieces. With right sides together, machine-stitch a short rectangle to each short end of the long rectangle. Press the seams open. With right sides together, machine-stitch one end of the zipper section to one raw end. Press the seam away from the zipper.

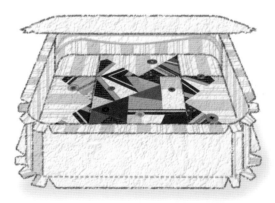

15 Cut a 17-in. square of striped silk. Pin the remaining length of piping around the edge of the right side of the square, in the same way as you did in Step 10.

16 Open the zipper. With right sides together, pin, baste, and machine-stitch the raw edge of the side panel to the bottom of the pillow. Cut notches in the seam allowance at each corner. Turn the pillow cover right side out, and insert the pillow form.

armchair throw

This small throw is a good-size project to make over a weekend. The wool pieces are covered here and there with floral chintz in autumn colors, which give the throw a warm, comforting feel. The same chintz fabric is used for the binding, which adds a sense of unity. The pieces are held together with embroidery stitches in red and ocher, colors that are picked out from the fabrics.

The finished throw measures 20 x 24 in.

½-in. seam allowances are included throughout.

YOU WILL NEED

▸ Pattern paper

▸ Pencil

▸ 25 x 35 in. piece of thin wool fabric

▸ 25 x 35 in. piece of thin printed cotton fabric

▸ Embroidery floss

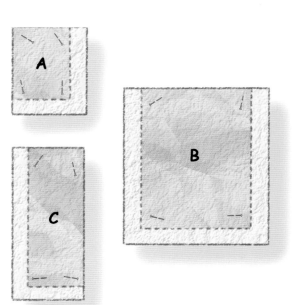

1 On pattern paper, draw your design and label each piece with a letter.

2 Cut out the individual pattern pieces, adding 1 in. to all internal edges. Pin your pattern pieces to the wool fabric and cut them out. Some pieces will be covered by printed fabric, so cut out the appropriate printed pieces, too.

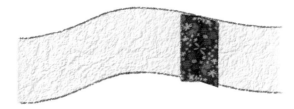

5 From the remaining printed fabric, cut strips 2 in. wide on the short grain. Join them together to make a strip long enough to go all around the quilt. (See page 119.)

6 Fold under ½ in. along each long edge of the strip and press.

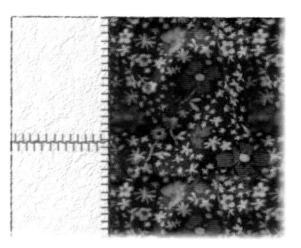

3 Baste the cotton pieces to the corresponding wool pieces. On each internal edge, turn under a ½-in. hem; baste or press. Turn under a second ½-in. hem; press. (To miter a hemmed corner, open out the second hem on both edges, and fold in the corner diagonally, so that the pressed creases align; press. Trim off the corner, leaving ¼ in., and refold the second hem on each side.) Slipstitch the hems and the miter.

4 Referring to your pattern, hand-stitch the pieces together, using embroidery floss and a variation on Cretan stitch. (See page 119.) Remove the basting stitches.

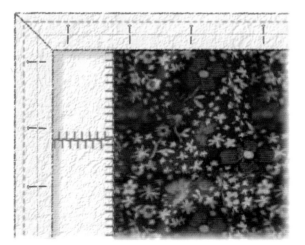

7 Open out the folds. With right sides together, pin the strip around the edge of the throw, aligning the raw edges and mitering the corners. (See page 120.) Machine-stitch along the first fold line.

8 Fold the binding over to the back of the throw, fold along the remaining fold line, and pin the binding in place, again mitering the corners. Slipstitch all around by hand. (See page 116.)

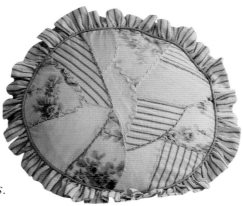

circular pillow

To make this circular pillow, I used a selection of pale silks. The ruffle around the edge softens any hard edges.

One of the fabrics I found for this is a print designed to look like an ikat weave, a process that involves tie-dyeing the yarn before it is woven. The colors have a waterlike quality. The colors of the embroidery floss pick up the colors of the fabric.

The color scheme is neutral, which makes the pillow suitable for most settings. Use it in a living room or as an accent in a bedroom.

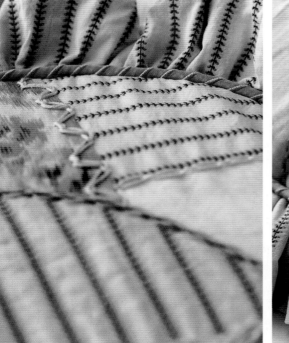

The finished pillow measures 18 in. in diameter. ½-in. seam allowances are included throughout.

YOU WILL NEED

- Cardstock or template plastic
- Pencil
- 16-in. square of muslin for foundation fabric
- 1 yd. linen
- Scraps of silks
- Embroidery floss in three pale shades
- 5 x 26-in. strip of silk for the ruffle
- Two 52-in. lengths of fabric-covered piping cord
- 10-in. zipper
- Circular pillow form 15 in. in diameter

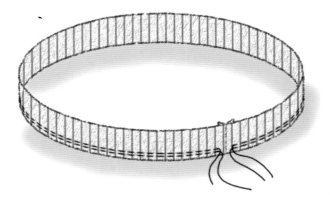

1 Draw and cut out a circle of cardstock or template plastic 16 in. in diameter. Draw around it on the foundation fabric and the linen, adding no seam allowances, and cut out one piece from each fabric. Following the instructions on pages 114–116, cover the foundation fabric with crazy patchwork silk scraps, sewing some of the curved seams by hand and using a machine-stitch when the seams are straight. Embroider over the hand-sewn curved seams with a cable chain stitch and a cable zigzag stitch, varying the color of the embroidery floss for each row. (See page 118.)

2 With right sides together, machine-stitch the two short ends of the silk strip together. Fold the strip in half lengthwise, with the seam on the inside. Press the fold and hand-stitch two parallel rows of running stitches ¼ in. and ½ in. from the raw edge, leaving the thread ends loose.

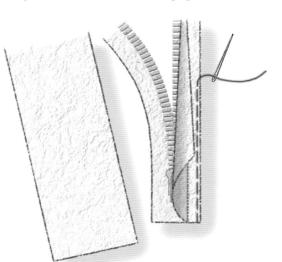

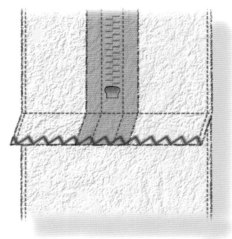

5 For the zipper section, cut two 2 x 11-in. pieces of linen. Following the instructions on page 121, insert an invisible zipper.

6 For the side gusset, cut one 3 x 38-in. piece of linen. With right sides together, machine-stitch one short end of this piece to one short end of the zipper section. Zigzag-stitch the two raw edges of the seam together and press away from the zipper section.

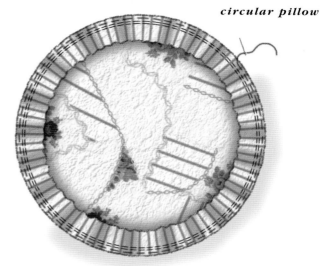

3 Pin and then machine-stitch one length of piping to the right side of the pillow top, with the raw edges facing outward and aligning with the raw edges of the pillow top. (See page 120.) Cut small notches in the piping seam allowances to ease the piping around the curve.

4 Gently pull the threads of the two rows of running stitches to gather the ruffle to the circumference of the pillow top. Pin and then baste the ruffle to the right side of the pillow top, with the raw edges aligning with the raw edges of the pillow and the ruffle facing inward. Machine-stitch the ruffle in place, stitching close to the stitching line on the piping.

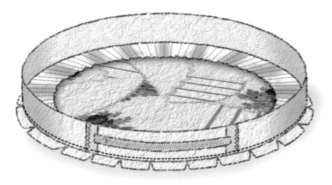

7 With right sides together and aligning the raw edges, baste and then machine-stitch the side gusset to the top of the pillow, cutting small notches in the side gusset at regular intervals to ease it around the curve. Machine-stitch the raw short end of the side gusset to the raw short end of the zipper section. Zigzag-stitch the two raw edges of the seam together and press away from the zipper section.

8 Pin and then machine-stitch the remaining length of piping to the right side of the linen circle cut in Step 1, in the same way as you did in Step 3. Open the zipper. With right sides together, pin and then machine-stitch the back of the pillow to the raw edge of the side gusset, in the same way as you did in Step 7. Turn the pillow cover right side out and insert the pillow form.

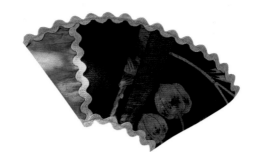

silk fan pillow

*Crazy patchwork reached its height of popularity during
Victorian times when, coincidentally, there was also huge
enthusiasm for all things Japanese. This project, with its colorful
fans, harks back to the same tradition. Here, however, I've given it
a contemporary twist by outlining the fans with beige rickrack
braid, so that they stand out against the background fabric.*

The finished pillow
measures approx.
16 in. square.

½-in. seam allowances are
included throughout.

YOU WILL NEED

▶ Cardstock for templates

▶ 2/3 yd. muslin for
foundation fabric

▶ Five different-colored silk
and coordinating fabrics
for the patchwork

▶ 5½ yd. rickrack braid

▶ Two 12 x 17-in.
pieces of linen for the
back of the pillow

▶ 16-in. square pillow form

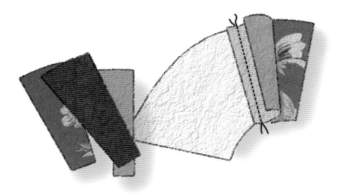

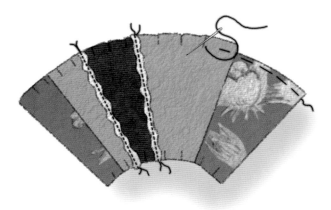

1 Make a cardstock pattern from template A on page 124. Pin the pattern to the foundation fabric and cut four pieces. Cut the assorted silks into wedge shapes of varying widths. Following the instructions on pages 114–116, cover the foundation pieces with crazy patchwork.

2 Machine-stitch lengths of rickrack braid over some of the seams. Make ½-in. cuts around each curved edge. Turn under these raw edges and baste them.

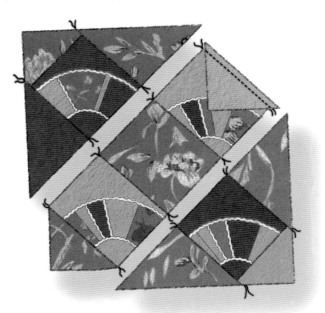

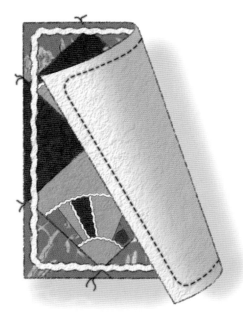

5 Using templates B and C on page 124 and adding ½ in. all around, cut four large and four small triangles from the fabrics used for the patchwork. Lay the blocks out in the required order, so that they form a large square. Machine-stitch them into three strips and press the seams open. Then machine-stitch the three strips together to complete the top of the pillow. Press the seams open.

6 Cut a square of foundation fabric that is the same size as the patchwork and baste it to the wrong side of the patchwork. Pin, baste, and machine-stitch the rickrack braid all around the right side of the patchwork ½ in. from the outer edge, stitching along the center of the braid and curving it around the corners.

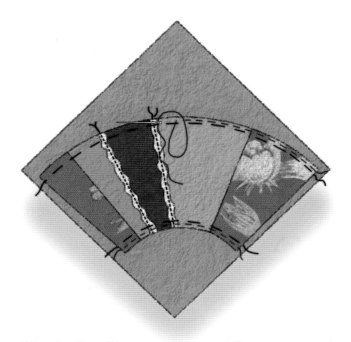

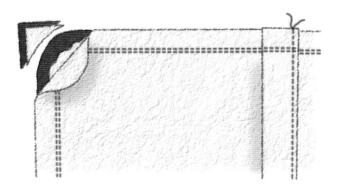

3 Cut four 6½-in. squares from different prints and solid-colored cottons. Appliqué the crazy patchwork fans to the squares by working running stitches close to the edges. Trim the patchwork to the same size as the foundation squares, if necessary. Remove the basting stitches.

4 Baste, and then machine-stitch lengths of rickrack braid over the curved edges of all of the fan shapes.

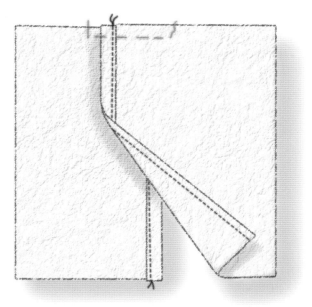

7 Cut two 12 x 17-in. pieces of linen. Fold under ½ in. along one long edge of each piece, press, and fold under a further ½ in. Pin, and then machine-stitch the fold in place. Overlap the hemmed edges by 5 in. and baste together.

8 With right sides together, baste the front of the pillow to the back. Machine-stitch all around, following the line of stitching on the rickrack braid. Trim the corners and turn the cover right side out. Insert the pillow form.

lampshade

Very often, decorative lampshade bases are finished with a plain shade. I hope this lampshade inspires you to make one that is more attractive.

The irregular pattern of patchwork shapes and the open Cretan stitch embroidery are contained within a border, which creates a sophisticated-looking balance.

Use lightweight silks for this project, because the fabric is gathered and you need to avoid bulk. I used scraps of silk from old ties because I like the way the jacquard weave catches the light during the day when the lamp is not in use.

The finished lampshade is 9 in. high, with a base 10 in. in diameter.

½-in. seam allowances are included throughout.

YOU WILL NEED

- Strips of different patterned colored silks, some from old ties

- 5 x 50-in. piece of muslin for foundation fabric

- Embroidery floss in coordinating color

- 14 x 50-in. piece of neutral-colored fabric for top of shade

- 1½ yd. lace edging

- 5 x 50-in. piece of silk fabric for backing

- Neutral-colored fabric lampshade 7½ in. high, with a base 10 in. in diameter

- 1 yd. ribbon at least ½ in. wide

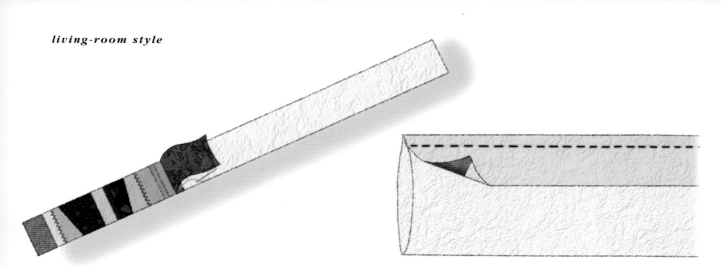

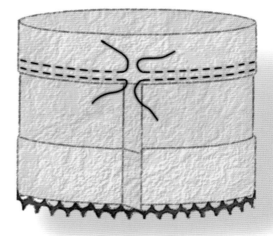

1 Following the instructions on page 114–116 and working from one side of the fabric to the other, sew randomly shaped pieces of silk to the strip of muslin foundation fabric. Work open Cretan stitch over some of the seams in a coordinating color of embroidery floss. (See page 118.)

2 Fold the piece of neutral-colored fabric for the top of the shade in half lengthwise and press. Baste along the unfolded long edge. Right sides together, pin or baste the crazy patchwork strip to the basted edge, and machine-stitch. Press the seam toward the crazy patchwork.

5 Fold under the raw edge of the silk by ½ in., press, and slipstitch it in place. (See page 116.) Press the whole piece flat.

6 Join the two short edges of the piece together with a French seam (see page 121), forming a cylinder shape. With the lace edging at the bottom, turn 2 in. to the wrong side at the top; press. Hand-stitch two parallel lines of running stitches 1¼ in. and 1¾ in. from the top, leaving the thread ends loose.

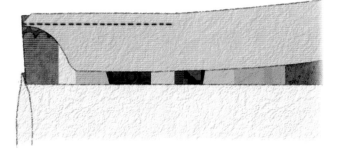

3 Pin the lace edging to the other long edge of the crazy patchwork, ½ in. from the edge, and machine-stitch.

4 Right sides together, pin the strip of silk backing fabric along the raw edge of the crazy patchwork and machine-stitch, stitching as close to the stitching line of the lace edging as possible. Press open the seam and fold the silk over to the back of the crazy patchwork. Press the edge.

7 Fit the cover over the lampshade, with the crazy patchwork border at the base of the shade. Carefully pull the running-stitch threads to gather the shade at the top, gathering it evenly. When the cover is gathered to the right size, knot the loose threads in a double knot.

8 Tie a ribbon around the gathers in a neat bow to finish.

❭ fruit bowl cover with beaded edging ❭ placemats and coasters ❭ tablecloth
❭ chair cover ❭ tabletop basket

kitchen pieces

fruit bowl cover with beaded edging

During Victorian times, this was a very decorative way of covering food bowls to protect the contents from flies during the summer months. In keeping with the tradition, one of the fabrics I have used is an antique lace sewn onto a cotton netting, which was originally the collar on a Victorian dress. The blue and cream silks that you can see underneath the netting are picked up by the shells and beads, which are used to weight the cover when it is in use.

YOU WILL NEED

- Cardstock or template plastic
- Pencil and tracing paper
- Pattern paper
- Scraps of muslin and lace netting for the patchwork
- Cream and blue silks to back the patchwork
- Dark and pale blue embroidery flosses
- Bias-cut strip of silk 2 in. wide x the circumference of your template plus 1 in.
- Large and small beads
- Large and small shells with a hole drilled in the top
- Strong cotton-wrapped polyester thread

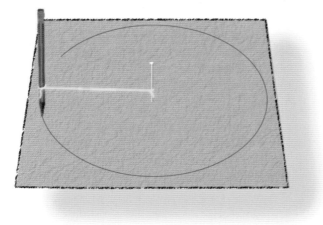

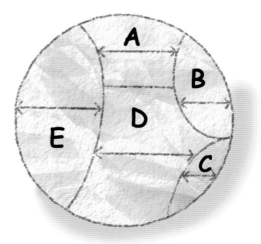

1 Measure the diameter of the bowl you want to cover and add at least 4 in. all around. Draw a circle to this measurement on cardstock or template plastic and cut it out.

2 Draw around the template on paper. Mark out the individual sections and label each one. Mark a horizontal arrow on each section. Cut out the individual pattern sections.

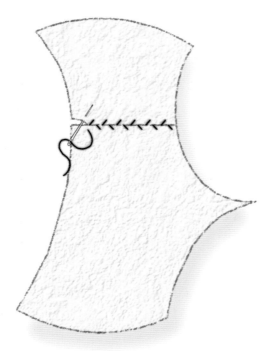

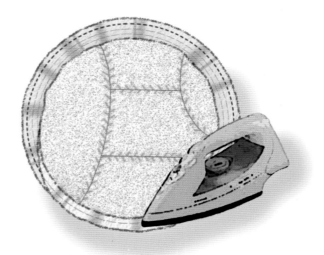

5 Using dark and pale blue embroidery floss, hand-stitch the sections together, using an antique faggot hem and making small stitches. (See page 119.)

6 Fold the strip of bias-cut fabric in half lengthwise, and press. Open the strip out again and fold in each long edge so that the raw edges meet the center pressed line. Press the folds, and open out the fabric. With right sides together, pin the strip around the outer edge of the cover, aligning the raw edges. Machine-stitch it in place along the first fold. Fold the binding over so that the next fold aligns with the raw edge of the cover.

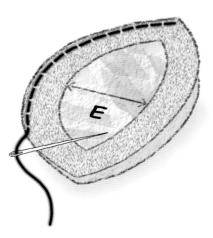

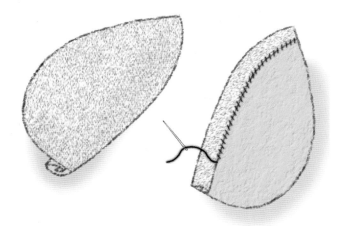

3 Aligning the arrows on the pattern pieces with the grain of the fabric, cut out the pieces from muslin or lace, adding 1 in. all around on each piece. Cut pieces of silk the same size—cream for the muslin and blue for the lace—and baste the corresponding silk and lace/muslin pieces together.

4 Apart from the outer edges, which will lie on the circumference of the food cover, fold over each edge of each piece by ½ in. twice and slipstitch it in place, mitering any corners to reduce the bulk. Press the seams flat.

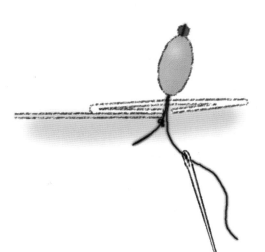

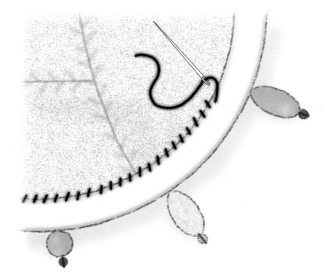

7 Thread a needle with strong thread, and bring the needle up through the fold to the top of the cover. Thread through a large bead, followed by a small bead, and pass the needle back through the large bead the other way. The small bead acts as a stopper. Take the needle back through the fold on the binding and make a double stitch underneath it close to the edge of the main piece. Attach more beads and the shells in the same way.

8 Fold the bias binding over to the back of the piece and slipstitch the last edge under, following the line of the last fold.

placemats
and coasters

A fine meal is definitely enhanced by a beautiful table setting,

and these placemats and coasters certainly help to set the mood.

The bright colors would be great for a children's party. Try to use

durable, washable fabrics and make the color combinations lively.

The finished placemats each measure 10 x 12¼ in. The finished coasters each measure 4 in. in diameter. ½-in. seam allowances are included throughout.

YOU WILL NEED

For one placemat:

- Seven 2¾ x10-in. strips of muslin for foundation fabric
- Scraps of fabric strips at least 2¾ in. wide for the crazy patchwork
- 1 yd. 2-in.-wide ribbon
- 10 x 13¼-in. piece of batting
- 1½ yd. piping
- 11 x 13¼-in. piece of cotton fabric for backing

For one coaster:

- Two 3 x 5-in. strips of muslin foundation fabric
- Strips of fabrics at least 3 in. wide
- Assorted ribbons
- 5-in. square of batting
- 14-in. length of piping
- Circle of cardstock 5 in. in diameter
- 5-in. square of cotton for backing

making a placemat

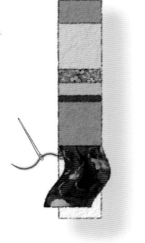

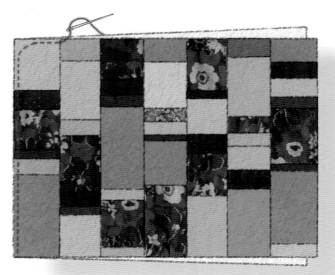

1 Cut your crazy patchwork scraps into pieces at least 2¾ in. wide and of varying lengths. Following the instructions on pages 114–116 and working from one end of the foundation strips to the other, cover the strips with crazy patchwork, occasionally inserting a length of ribbon between the pieces. (See page 116.) Continue until you have covered all seven foundation strips with crazy patchwork.

2 Machine-stitch the seven crazy patchwork strips together lengthwise and press open the seams. Place the assembled patchwork right side up on top of the batting, and baste the pieces together.

5 Trim off the corners and cut small notches around them to reduce the bulk.

6 Turn the placemat right side out and slipstitch the opening closed. (See page 116.) Press the placemat flat.

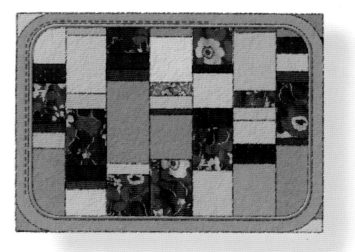

3 With the raw edges of the piping facing outward, pin and then machine-baste the piping all around the right side of the patchwork top ½ in. from the edge. Gently curve the piping around the corners, cutting small notches in the piping seam allowances on the curves.

4 With right sides together, machine-stitch the cotton backing fabric to the top of the placemat, stitching as close as possible to the piping, leaving an opening in one side.

making a coaster

1 Cover two strips of muslin with crazy patchwork, as in Step 1 of the placemat. Machine-stitch the two strips together along one long edge, and press open the seam. Place the patchwork right side up on top of the batting, and baste the pieces together.

2 Using a cardstock template, cut a 5-in. circle from the patchwork and batting and another from the square of backing cotton. Pipe the edge of the patchwork circle as in Step 3, attach the backing circle as in Step 4, and complete the coaster as in Steps 5 and 6.

tablecloth

This project came about when I found some antique, yellow printed fabric from France. The fabric brought to mind atmospheric Parisian cafés, which inspired me to make it into a tablecloth.

The yellow fabric determined the color and texture of the other fabrics in the design. I decorated the border with brightly colored ribbon and fresh white lace and linen, along with some subdued tones and striped fabric to highlight these details.

The finished tablecloth measures 60 in. in diameter. ½-in. seam allowances are included throughout.

YOU WILL NEED

- ▶ Pencil and string
- ▶ Pattern paper
- ▶ 1¾ yd. good-quality white linen for main tablecloth center and backing
- ▶ 3½ yd. muslin for foundation fabric
- ▶ Scraps of cotton fabric at least 12 in. in length for border
- ▶ Strips of fabric 12–24 in. long and 2 in. wide, cut on the bias
- ▶ Pieces of lace edging, 12–24 in. in length (optional)
- ▶ 12–24-in. lengths of military ribbon
- ▶ Bias binding

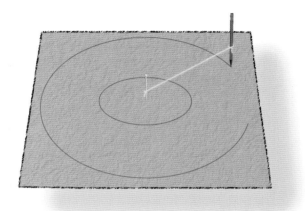

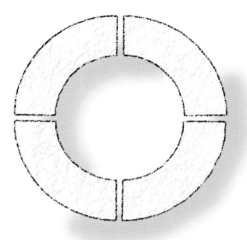

1 Tie a pencil to one end of a piece of string. Pin the other end to the center of a large piece of paper. Adjusting the length of the string as necessary, draw two concentric circles—one 36 in. in diameter, and the other 60 in. in diameter. Cut around the edge of the outer circle. Pin the pattern to white linen and cut it out.

2 Now cut out the inner circle of the pattern paper and discard the central portion. Cut the remaining paper into four parts that are roughly the same size. Pin the four pattern pieces to the foundation fabric and cut them out, adding ½ in. to each straight edge for the seam allowance.

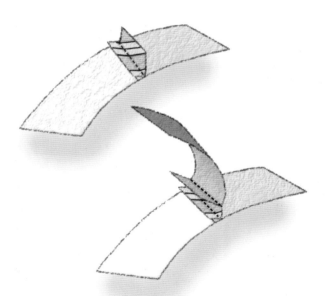

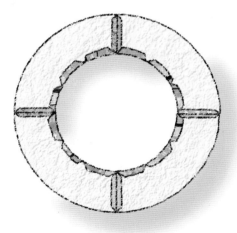

5 To cover the edges with bias-cut fabric, place the bias strip on top of the first patchwork piece and machine-stitch ½ in. from the outer edge. Flip the bias strip over and press. With right sides together, place the next patchwork piece on top of the bias strip, aligning the outer edges, and machine-stitch ½ in. from the edge. Flip the patchwork piece over to the right side. Continue, covering the edges of the patchwork pieces with either ribbon or bias-cut fabric, until you have covered all the foundation fabric.

6 If you wish, appliqué strips of lace over some sections. (See page 116.) With right sides together, machine-stitch the four crazy patchwork segments into a ring. Press open the seams. Cut small notches around the edge of the inner circle, fold the fabric under by ½ in., and press.

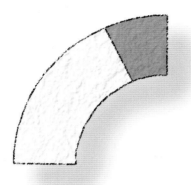

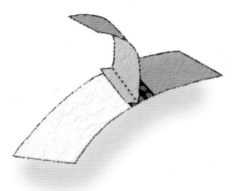

3 Cut your crazy patchwork scraps into pieces at least 12 in. long and of varying widths, cutting the sides at different angles. Place the first piece in position on the foundation fabric. The edges will be covered by ribbon or bias-cut fabric.

4 To cover the edges with ribbon, place the ribbon over one edge of the patchwork fabric and machine-stitch down one edge to secure the patchwork fabric in place. With the right side of the fabric facing down, place the next patchwork piece over the other edge of the ribbon and stitch it. Fold the patchwork piece to the right side and press; half the ribbon should be visible between the pieces.

7 Place the crazy patchwork border right side up on the circle of linen that you cut out in Step 1. Pin or baste around the outer edge to hold the border in place. Slipstitch around the inner edge. (See page 116.)

8 Cover the outer edge of the tablecloth with bias binding. (See pages 119–120.)

chair cover

This tie-on cover provides a decorative finish to the back and seat of a simple kitchen chair. The striped fabric was taken from a vintage slipcover and combined with faded chintz that was originally used for curtains. Although the fabrics are old, the cover would not look out of place in a contemporary setting.

The backrest and seat of the chair that we used were the same width, but if they are different on your chair, average the two measurements to calculate the width of fabric you will need.

½-in. seam allowances are included throughout.

YOU WILL NEED

- Muslin for foundation fabric
- Small pieces of chintz and striped fabrics and a solid-colored cotton for the crazy patchwork
- Strip of chintz fabric 6½ in. wide x 2.5 times the length of the outside edges for the ruffle
- Piping the length of the outside edges of the chair cover plus 1 in.
- 12 3 x 14½-in. strips of fabric for ties
- Linen in a coordinating color to back the chair cover

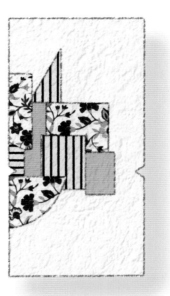

1 Measure the length of the backrest plus the depth of the seat, and the width of the seat. Add ½ in. all around for the seam allowance and cut a piece of foundation fabric to these measurements. Mark the point where the backrest meets the back of the chair seat by cutting a small notch on either side of the fabric.

2 Cut pieces of chintz, striped, and solid-colored fabrics in different shapes and sizes, and arrange them on the foundation fabric to work out how to overlap them. Starting in the center, baste your first patchwork piece to the foundation fabric. One edge of the next piece will overlap one edge of the basted piece, and this edge needs to be finished. Fold under and press this edge, overlap it on the piece that is already basted to the foundation fabric, and baste it in place. Machine-stitch along the folded-under edge, stitching close to the edge. Continue adding pieces in this way until you have covered the foundation fabric.

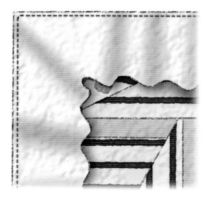

5 With right sides together, baste the piping around the edges of the patchwork, aligning the raw edges. Machine-stitch the piping in place, stitching as close as possible to the cord. (See page 120.) Cut a small notch in the piping seam allowances at each corner to allow it to fit around the corner.

6 With right sides together and the raw edges even, pin the ruffle to the chair cover around all four sides. You may have to adjust the gathers in order to get it to fit exactly. Baste, then machine-stitch the ruffle to the chair cover, following the stitching line of the piping.

3 With right sides together, machine-stitch the two short ends of the ruffle together. Press open the seam.

4 Fold the fabric in half lengthwise, right side out. Press the fold. Hand-stitch two parallel lines of running stitch around the ruffle ¼ in. apart, with the first line ¼ in. from the raw edge, leaving the thread ends loose. Gently pull the threads to gather the ruffle to roughly the same length as the outer edge of the patchwork.

7 Make the 12 strips of fabric into ties. (See page 121.) Pin and baste them to the right side of the patchwork, with the ties and ruffle facing inward and their raw edges even with the raw edges of the patchwork. Attach them 3 in. either side of the corners and 1½ in. either side of the notches cut in Step 1.

8 Cut a piece of linen the same size as the patchwork. With right sides together, baste and then machine-stitch the linen to the patchwork, leaving an 8-in. opening in one side. Cut a notch at each corner, turn the cover right side out, and slipstitch the opening closed. (See page 116.)

tabletop basket

The fabrics that I used here are scraps from dresses that my mother and grandmother made many years ago. Strong machine-stitching forms the sides of the basket, which are tied in pretty bows. I chose to make a feature of the stitching by using a thicker thread in a contrasting color.

The hand-embroidered blanket stitch that covers the seams between the pieces of crazy patchwork is an integral part of the patchwork, almost dominating the basket.

The finished basket measures 8 x 10 x 2 in.

YOU WILL NEED

- Scraps of various cotton prints and solid-colored fabrics for the crazy patchwork
- 12 x 14-in. piece of muslin for foundation fabric
- Embroidery floss in contrasting colors
- 12 x 14-in. piece of batting
- 12 x 14-in. piece of cotton fabric for backing
- Vanishing fabric marker pen
- Eight 1¼ x 8-in. strips of fabric for ties
- 2 x 53-in. strip of cotton fabric cut on the bias

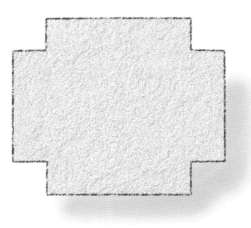

1 Cut the scraps of printed cotton into random shapes. Following the instructions on pages 114–116 and working from one side of the fabric to the other, cover the foundation fabric with crazy patchwork. Blanket-stitch over the seams, using contrasting colors of embroidery floss. (See page 117.)

2 Cut a 2-in. square out of each corner of the piece of batting to reduce the bulk.

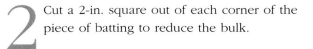

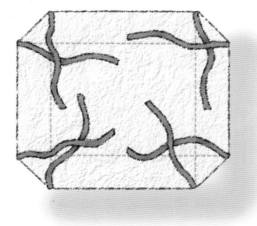

5 Cut off the corners on the diagonal, taking care not to cut into the lines of machine-stitching.

6 Make eight ties. (See page 121.) Position one pair of ties at each corner, aligning with the lines of machine-stitching, with the ties facing inward. Baste in position.

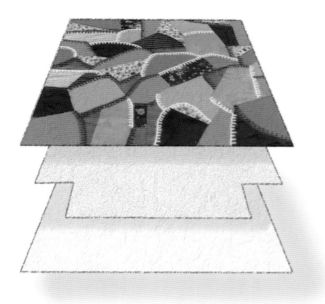

3 Place the backing piece right side down on your work surface, with the batting on top and the crazy patchwork right side up on top of the batting. Working from the center outward, pin through all three layers to hold them together and baste around the edges, stitching through all layers.

4 Using a vanishing fabric marker, draw a line along each side of the fabric approximately 2 in. from the edge. Shorten the stitch length and topstitch along these lines in a contrasting color.

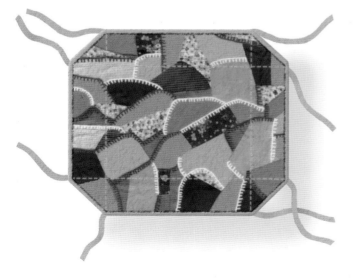

7 Cover the edges of the basket with bias binding. (See page 120.) With the backing fabric on top, fold and press along the machine-stitched lines to make the sides of the basket.

8 Tie each pair of ties in a neat bow to hold the sides of the basket in place and provide an attractive finishing touch.

◗ cosmetics case ◗ jewelry box ◗ laundry bag
◗ blanket with crazy patchwork border ◗ bolster ◗ quilt tied with rosettes
◗ dressing-table runner ◗ pillowcase ◗ scented sachet

in the bedroom

cosmetics case

This is an unusual shape for a cosmetics case. I took my inspiration from the segments of an orange, but the patchwork pieces do not follow a strict pattern around the semicircle. This randomness is what I love about crazy patchwork. The star-shaped embroidery stitch highlights the uneven size of the strips of fabric.

The finished case measures approx. 4 x 5½ x 11 in.
½-in. seam allowances are included throughout.

YOU WILL NEED

▶ Compass and pencil
▶ 12-in. square of pattern paper
▶ 6½ x 24-in. piece of muslin for foundation fabric
▶ Solid-colored cotton and chintz strips at least 6½ in. long and 2–4 in. wide
▶ Embroidery floss in two colors
▶ ⅛ yd. waterproof lining fabric
▶ Two 29½-in. lengths of piping cord covered in a chintz fabric
▶ 8-in. zipper
▶ 6 x 30 in. piece of colored cotton fabric

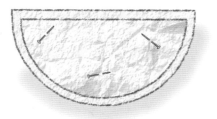

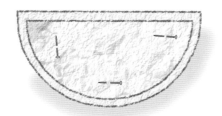

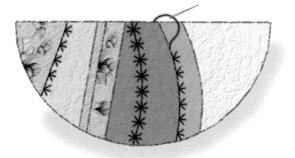

1 Draw a circle 11 in. in diameter on pattern paper. Divide the circle in half and cut out two semicircles to use as patterns. Pin the pattern pieces to the foundation fabric and cut out one piece from each pattern, adding a ½-in. seam allowance all around on each piece.

2 Following the instructions on pages 114–116 and working from one side of the foundation fabric to the other, cover the two semicircles with crazy patchwork, varying the width of the patchwork pieces. Embroider over some of the seams with a connected series of eight-pointed stars. Occasionally, work a line of half-stars, echoing the semicircular shape of the case.

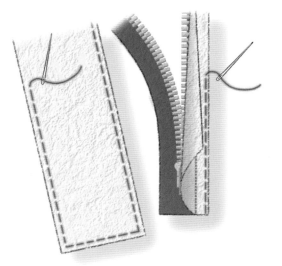

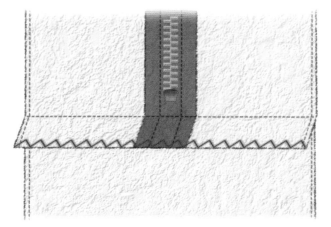

5 Cut two 3 x 9-in. pieces of colored cotton fabric and two pieces of lining fabric the same size. With wrong sides together, baste each piece of cotton to one piece of lining fabric. Following the instructions on page 121, insert an invisible zipper.

6 Cut a 5 x 21¼-in. piece of cotton and a piece of lining fabric the same size. With wrong sides together, baste the pieces together. With right sides together, machine-stitch one short edge to one short edge of the zipper section. Zigzag-stitch the raw edges of the seam allowance together and press away from the zipper.

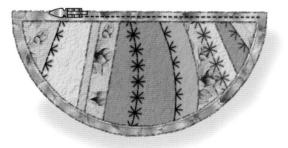

3 Using the pattern from Step 1 and adding a ½-in. seam allowance all around, cut two semicircles from your chosen lining fabric. With wrong sides together, baste one lining piece to each patchwork section.

4 Pin one length of fabric-covered piping around the edge of each semicircle on the right side, with the raw edge of the piping aligning with the edge of the semicircle. Using a piping foot or zipper foot on the machine, stitch the piping to the semicircle, stitching as close as possible to the cord. (See page 120.) Cut small notches in the piping seam allowances at each corner and on the curve.

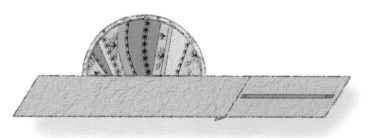

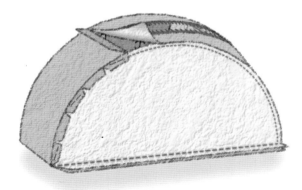

7 With right sides together, place the straight edge of one patchwork section in the center of one long side of the piece connected to the zipper in the previous step. Baste it in place, and pin the rest of the straight edge around the edge of the semicircle. Machine-stitch these sections together.

8 Machine-stitch the end of the zipper section to the end of the gusset. Zigzag-stitch the raw edges of the seam together and press away from the zipper. Open the zipper. With right sides together, pin, baste, and machine-stitch the remaining patchwork semicircle to the other edge of the gusset. Finish the raw edges with a zigzag stitch, and turn the bag right side out through the zipper opening.

jewelry box

Shoeboxes are great for storing trinkets that you do not want on permanent display. A simple cardboard box looks beautiful covered in fabric in a wonderful array of colors and textures.

To give the design continuity, I included among the patchwork fabrics some scraps of the striped fabric that I used for the base of the box. Adapt this idea for an attractive box storage system in a closet or on open shelves.

YOU WILL NEED

- Cardboard box
- Cardstock or template plastic
- Pencil
- Pattern paper
- Muslin for foundation fabric
- Striped fabric for the base
- Assorted fabrics in different colors for the patchwork
- Fusible web
- Assorted ribbons and lace at least ½ in. wide
- Fabric glue
- Printed lining paper

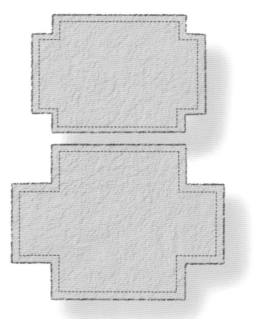

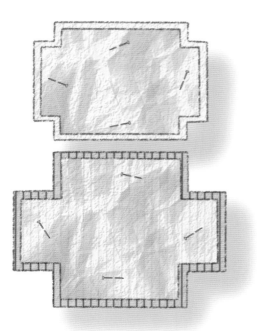

1 Measure the lid of the box, including the depth of the sides, and add ½ in. all around. Make a template from cardstock or template plastic. Make a template for the base of the box in the same way. Draw around the templates on pattern paper.

2 Pin the paper patterns to the relevant fabrics. Cut a piece of foundation fabric for the lid, adding ½ in. all around. Cut a piece of striped fabric for the base, again adding ½ in. all around.

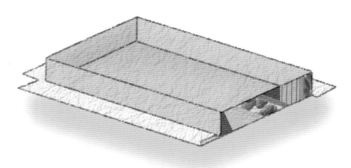

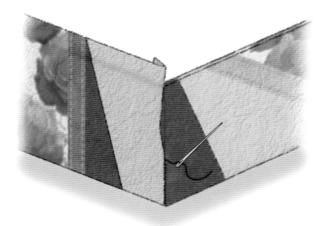

5 Spread fabric glue over the top of the lid and glue the patchwork to it. When the glue has dried, apply glue to one flap of the first corner and fold it around the corner, pressing it against the box to secure. Fold under the second flap on this corner by ½ in. so that it aligns with the corner.

6 Slipstitch the second flap in place at the corner. (See page 116.) Repeat this on the other three corners. Fold the remaining edges around to the inside of the lid and glue in place. Repeat Steps 5 and 6 to cover the base of the box with the striped fabric.

3 Roughly plan the shapes and sizes of each of the crazy patchwork pieces for the lid, fitting them together like a jigsaw puzzle. Following the manufacturer's instructions, iron fusible web to the wrong side of the fabric. Carefully peel off the backing paper from each piece and iron them in place on the foundation fabric, so that the edges connect as closely as possible.

4 Using matching threads, machine-stitch the ribbons and lace over the seams, stitching close to each outer edge of the ribbons and lace. (See page 116.)

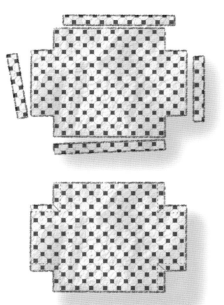

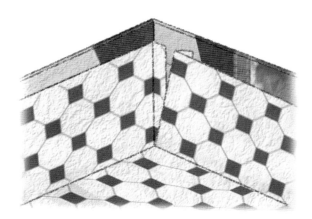

7 Draw around the templates that you made for the lid and base on printed lining paper and cut 1 in. off each side flap. At each corner, make a small cut at a 45° angle within the seam allowance.

8 Glue the lining pieces inside the box lid and base, covering the raw edges of the fabrics, gluing and folding the flaps in the same way as described in Steps 5 and 6.

laundry bag

I designed this laundry bag with a sunny bedroom in mind—perhaps a child's nursery with a lively color scheme. The bright hues of yellow and orange-pink in a windmill-like patchwork are very buoyant. The embroidery I have chosen—a crossed buttonhole stitch—has a pretty naivety about it. It goes well with the nostalgic 1950s printed fabric that dominates the bag.

Of course, you could tone down the color scheme and reduce the scale of the embroidery stitches to give the bag a more sophisticated look. When you're making a project for a specific room, always bear the character of that room in mind.

The finished bag measures 17½ x 29¼ in. ½-in. seam allowances are included throughout.

YOU WILL NEED

- ⅓ yd. muslin for foundation fabric
- ⅔ yd. printed fabric
- Scraps of cotton prints for the crazy patchwork
- Embroidery floss in different colors
- 1 yd. lining fabric in a coordinating color
- 2 yd. cord

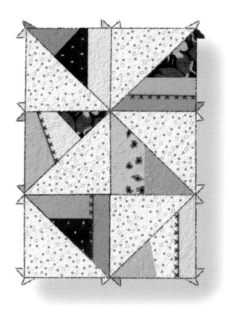

1 Using template A on page 122 and adding a ½-in. seam allowance all around, cut six triangles each from the foundation fabric and cotton prints, aligning the short edges with the grain of the fabric. Cover the foundation-fabric triangles from one corner to the other with crazy patchwork pieces. Pin the first crazy patchwork piece right side up on the triangle, with the next piece right side down along the raw edge of the first piece. Machine-stitch this piece in place. Fold it over to the right side, press in place, and add the next piece in the same way. Work crossed buttonhole stitch over some of the seams on the crazy patchwork. (See page 117.)

2 Alternating crazy patchwork and cotton-print fabric triangles as shown, machine-stitch four triangles together to make a rectangle and press open the seams. Make two more rectangles in the same way. Machine-stitch the three rectangles together to complete the front of the bag. Press open the seams between the rows.

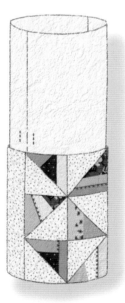

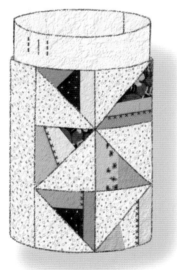

5 Machine-stitch two 1-in. lines parallel with the center seam 1 in. from each side of the opening.

6 Fold the lining inside the bag, leaving 2¼ in. protruding. Baste along the fold line to secure. Machine-stitch two lines around the lining, even with the top and bottom of the opening, starting and finishing at the two stitched lines parallel to the center seam.

3 From the print fabric, cut an 18½ x 27¼-in. rectangle for the back of the bag. From the lining fabric, cut two 18½ x 33¼-in. rectangles. With right sides together, machine-stitch one lining piece to the patchwork front of the bag along one short edge, and the remaining lining piece to the back of the bag.

4 Right sides together, machine-stitch the front of the bag to the back along the long edges, leaving a 1-in. opening on one side 1 in. above the seam between the lining and the front piece. Press open the seams and turn the bag right side out.

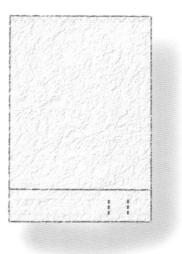

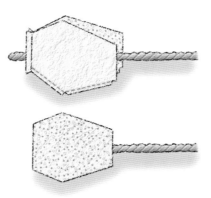

7 Turn the bag wrong side out. Machine-stitch across the base of the bag and zigzag-stitch the raw edge. Turn the bag right side out.

8 Using template B on page 122, cut two solid-colored and two print pieces of fabric. With right sides together, with the cord sandwiched between them, machine-stitch one solid-colored piece to one print piece along the bottom, stitching across the cord to secure it. Working by hand, backstitch along one side as shown. Clip notches in the seam allowance, turn the piece right side out, and slipstitch the opening closed. Thread the uncovered end of the cord through the channel in the bag, then cover the other end of the cord in the same way.

blanket with crazy patchwork border

Solid-colored woolen blankets can look very dull. The temptation is to fold them up and hide them away in a closet when they're not in use. This blanket, with its deep border of crazy patchwork, is striking enough to be on permanent display and makes a bold design statement in a simple, neutral-colored bedroom.

The finished blanket measures approx. 73 x 89 in. ½-in. seam allowances are included throughout.

YOU WILL NEED

- Woolen blanket
- 2¼ yd. muslin for foundation fabric
- Different cotton and wool fabrics for the squares, some in solid colors, some printed
- Scraps of printed brocades
- Military ribbon
- Embroidery floss in at least two colors
- Silk ribbons ¼–½ in. wide in two colors
- Two 9 x 57-in. strips of solid-colored cotton fabric for border backing
- Two 9 x 89-in. strips of solid-colored cotton fabric for border backing
- 9¼ yd. x 2-in.-wide bias binding

1 Cut the blanket to 57 x 73 in., trimming off the edging all the way around. Cut the foundation fabric into 36 9-in. squares.

2 Following the instructions on pages 114–116, cover the cotton foundation squares with crazy patchwork, using at least three different fabrics on each square, in a patchwork made up from at least four to five pieces. Occasionally insert a piece of military ribbon between the seams. (See page 116.)

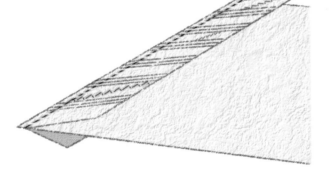

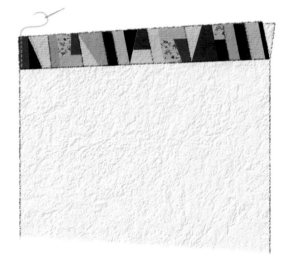

5 Lay one short border backing strip on the floor, right side up, with one short edge of the blanket on top. Place a strip of seven patchwork squares right side down on top of the short edge of the blanket, and check that the edges of all three layers align. Baste, and then machine-stitch the three layers together, stitching ½ in. from the edge. Repeat on the opposite edge of the blanket.

6 Fold back the patchwork and backing strips and press in place. Baste the patchwork and backing layers together along the remaining raw edges.

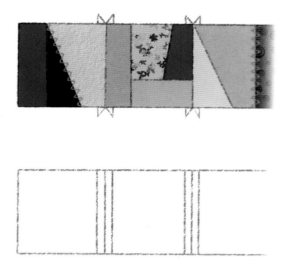

3 Using embroidery floss, couch ribbon over some of the seams in a zigzag pattern, using large stitches. (See page 118.) Occasionally couch a straight line of ribbon, angling the stitches.

4 Right sides together, machine-stitch the squares together to make two rows of seven squares and two rows of 11 squares. Press open the seams.

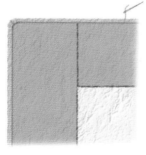

7 Repeat Steps 5 and 6 on the long edges of the blanket.

8 Matching the raw edges, pin, then machine-stitch the binding to the right side of the blanket, mitering the corners and stitching ½ in. from the edge. (See page 120.) Fold the binding over to the back of the blanket. Fold under the raw edge of the binding by ½ in. and press the fold. Pin, then slipstitch the binding in place, mitering the corners. Press the binding flat.

bolster

I choose a very elaborate-looking patchwork pattern for this piece. (It's less complicated to make than it appears.) Rich fabrics such as deep pinks and turquoise satin fabrics create a rather decadent mood. Alternatively, you could use similar-colored fabrics with very different textures, such as herringbone tweeds alongside a solid silk of the same color. Whatever you choose, the surface becomes an interesting kaleidoscope of texture and color.

The finished bolster measures 6½ x 18 in. ½-in. seam allowances are included throughout.

YOU WILL NEED

- 1½ yd. muslin for foundation fabric
- Scraps of solid-colored cotton fabric, cotton prints, and silks
- 18¾ x 25¾-in. piece of muslin to back the patchwork
- 1¼ yd. piping cord covered in coordinating colored silk
- Two 21½ x 22½-in. pieces of white silk or good-quality linen
- Two 1-yd. lengths of ⅜-in.-wide bias-cut fabric or ¼-in.-wide ribbon for ties
- 6½ x 18-in. bolster pillow form

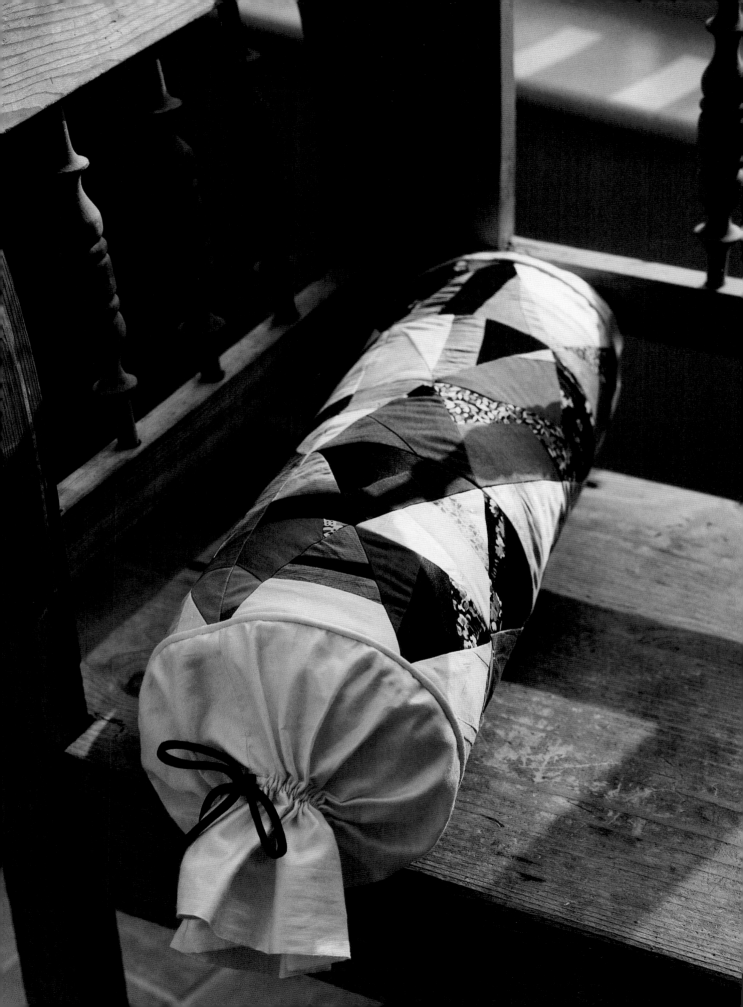

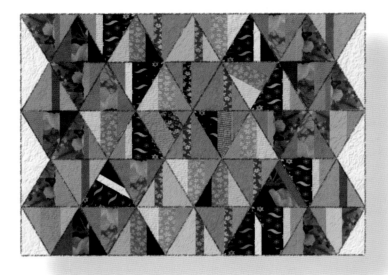

1 Using the template on page 122, cut 55 triangles from the foundation fabric, adding ½ in. all around on each piece. Following the instructions on pages 114–116, cover each triangle with crazy patchwork, using two or three scraps of fabric on each triangle. Trim the patchwork even with the edges of each foundation triangle.

2 With right sides together, machine-stitch 11 triangles together in a row and press open the seams. Repeat four times to make five rows. Machine-stitch the five rows together and press open the seams between the rows.

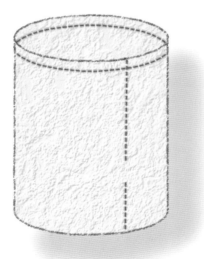

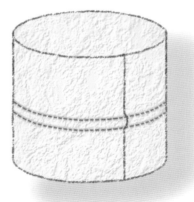

5 To make one end of the bolster cover, press under a double ½-in. hem along one short edge of one silk or linen piece, and machine-stitch. With right sides together, machine-stitch the long edges of the piece together, leaving a ½-in. opening 4 in. from the unhemmed end. Press open the seam. Repeat to make the second end with the other piece.

6 Turn the silk or linen cylinder right side out. Fold the fabric on the hemmed end of each cylinder to the inside, leaving 8 in. above the opening in the seam; press. Machine-stitch two parallel lines around each cylinder ½ in. apart, aligning with the top and bottom of the opening in the seam.

3 Baste the patchwork to a piece of muslin. Mark a vertical line through the center of the triangles on each short side, then trim each short edge ½ in. beyond this line to allow for the seam allowance.

4 With right sides together, machine-stitch the two short edges together. Press open the seam. Turn the cylinder right side out. Pin and machine-stitch piping around the two open ends of the bolster cover, ½ in. from each end, with the raw edges of the piping facing outward. (See page 120.)

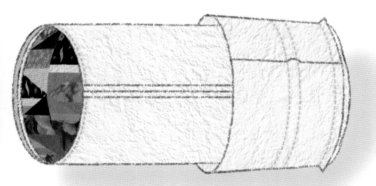

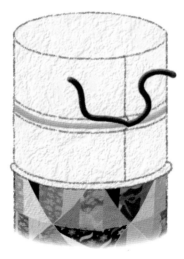

7 With the patchwork right side out, place one silk or linen cylinder, wrong side out, over one end of the patchwork cylinder, with the raw edge even with the raw edges of the piping, and the seams aligning. Machine-stitch, following the stitching lines of the piping. Repeat for the other end.

8 Turn both ends right side out, and insert the pillow form. Make two ties (see page 121), or cut two 1-yd. lengths of ribbon. Insert one tie or ribbon into the opening in the seam at each end of the bolster cover, threading it between the two parallel lines of stitching. Pull the ties or ribbons to gather up the ends, and tie them in bows.

quilt tied with rosettes

This quilt alternates crazy patchwork and solid squares. The diagonal lines of the crazy patchwork create a dynamic, striking design. The solid squares are made from a red chintz cotton with a strong yellow and turquoise floral design. These colors are picked up in the patchworked squares, unifying the whole quilt. The brown rosettes on each corner highlight the square block design of the quilt, and add a pretty detail.

The finished quilt measures 58½ x 70 in.

½-in. seam allowances are included throughout.

YOU WILL NEED

- 1¾ yd. muslin for foundation fabric
- Scraps of printed and solid-colored fabric cut to different widths
- 16 yd. ribbons 1–2 in. wide
- 15 12½-in. squares of printed fabric
- 60½ x 72-in. piece of backing fabric
- 58½ x 70-in. piece of medium-weight batting
- 20 uncovered metal buttons 1 in. in diameter

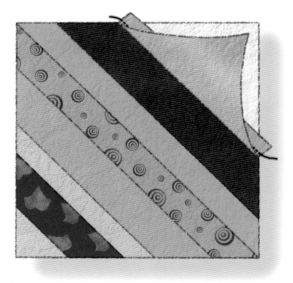

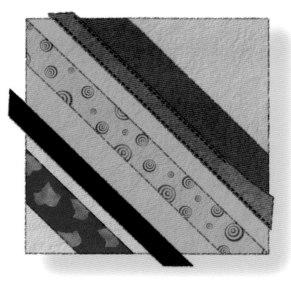

1 Cut the foundation fabric into 15 12½-in. squares. Following the instructions on pages 114–116, cover the foundation squares with crazy patchwork, sewing strips of fabric of varying widths diagonally across the squares.

2 Appliqué ribbons over the squares, following the diagonal lines and machine-stitching close to each edge of each ribbon. (See page 116.)

5 Cut 20 8-in. lengths of ribbon and join the short ends of each length with a French seam. (See page 121.) By hand, work running stitches along one edge of each ribbon, leaving the thread ends loose. Pull the threads to gather the ribbon into a rosette, and knot them to secure.

6 Following the manufacturer's instructions, cover each metal button with fabric or wide ribbon. Position one rosette at each point where four squares meet within the quilt. Place a covered button on top, and hand-stitch it in place, stitching through the rosette and the three layers of the quilt.

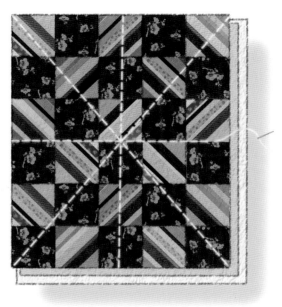

3 Alternating crazy patchwork and printed-fabric squares, machine-stitch the 30 squares together, right sides together, in six rows of five squares. Press open the seams. Machine-stitch the rows together, right sides together, aligning the seams from one row to the next. Press open the seams.

4 Lay the backing fabric right side down on a large, flat surface, and smooth out any wrinkles. Center the batting on top of the backing fabric and place the patchwork right side up on top of the batting. Working from the center outward, baste the layers together.

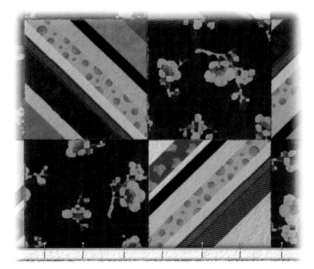

7 Fold the backing fabric over the batting and the quilt top, and fold under ½ in. so that you get a neat border all the way around. Pin in place.

8 Slipstitch the backing to the quilt top, removing the pins as you go and mitering the corners. (See page 120.)

dressing-table runner

In this piece, I wanted to focus attention on the embroidery, so I chose plain white fabrics in varying textures for the crazy patchwork. Some sections are unadorned white cotton, while others have intricate white, embroidered surfaces.

One of the two stitches I have chosen is very floral. Both stitches are sewn using embroidery floss that has been dip-dyed, which means that its rose hues vary in intensity.

The finished runner measures 15 x 24 in. ½-in. seam allowances are included throughout.

YOU WILL NEED

▶ White cotton fabrics of different textures, some plain, some embroidered

▶ 15 x 24 in. piece of muslin for the foundation fabric

▶ Soft brown, pink, and rose red embroidery flosses (dip dyed if possible)

▶ 17 x 26 in. piece of backing fabric

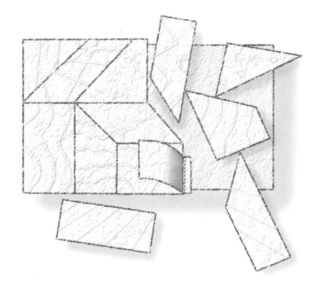

1 Cut the various white cotton fabrics into pieces of different shapes and sizes.

2 Position the patches on the foundation fabric, varying the texture from one patch to the next, and stitch them in place. (See pages 114–115.)

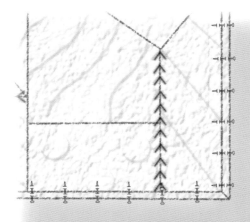

5 Place the backing fabric right side down on your work surface, and center the patchwork on top, right side up. Working diagonally from corner to corner, baste the layers together.

6 Fold each side of the backing fabric over by ½ in., and press. Then fold the backing fabric over the front of the patchwork to create a border, and pin in place.

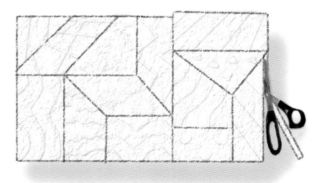

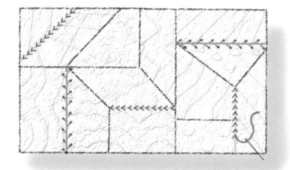

3 Press the piece flat and trim the patchwork to the same size as the foundation fabric.

4 Embroider some of the seams with rows of individual arrowhead stitch and Cretan stitch. (See pages 117 and 118.)

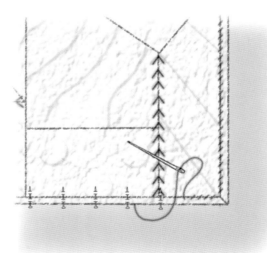

7 Slipstitch the border to the patchwork, mitering the corners. (See page 120.) Press flat.

pillowcase

This pillowcase would be wonderful as part of a set. You could make two or even four—and perhaps a border for a quilt, comforter, or duvet cover for even greater impact.

The freshness of the design means it looks great with crisp, white bed linen. The shiny silk ribbon embroidery that nestles among the pale tones of the patchwork is a subtle, but eye-catching, finishing touch.

The finished pillowcase measures 20 x 30 in. ½-in. seam allowances are included throughout.

YOU WILL NEED

- Two 4 x 31-in. strips of white cotton
- Two 4 x 21-in. strips of white cotton
- Scraps of solid-colored and print fabrics at least 4 in. long
- Large-eyed needle
- Silk ribbon ¼ in. wide for embroidery
- Scraps of lace braid at least 4 in. long
- 15 x 25-in. piece of cotton fabric for the top
- 21 x 31-in. piece of cotton fabric to back the patchwork
- 21 x 35-in. piece of cotton fabric for pillowcase back

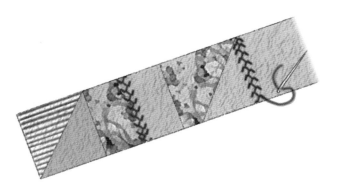

1 Following the instructions on pages 114–116, cover the white cotton strips with crazy patchwork. Using a large needle and thin silk ribbon, work Cretan stitch over some of the seams. (See page 118.)

2 Machine-appliqué the lace braid randomly over the crazy patchwork, covering the width of the patchwork strips, using thread in a matching color and stitching along each edge. (See page 116.)

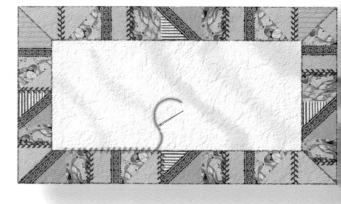

5 Fold under the inner edges of the border by ½ in. and press. At the corners, clip into the seam allowances so that they will lie flat.

6 Slipstitch the border to the piece of cotton for the top of the pillowcase. (See page 116.)

3 Trim the ends of each strip at 45-degree angles so that the corners will form neat miters.

4 With right sides together, machine-stitch the four strips together to make a rectangular border, leaving ½ in. unstitched at the inner end of each seam. Trim off the corners of the seam allowances even with the edges.

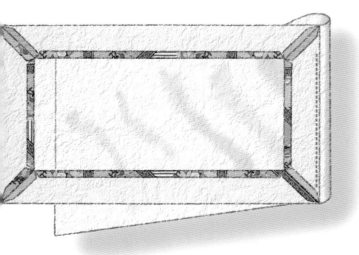

7 With right sides together, machine-stitch the patchwork to the backing fabric along one short edge. Press open the seam, fold the backing fabric to the back of the patchwork, and press.

8 Make a double hem at one end of the piece of cotton for the back of the pillowcase. (See page 121.) With right sides together, place the patchwork front on top of the pillowcase back, aligning the unstitched short edge of the patchwork and its backing with the unseamed short edge of the back. Fold the hemmed end of the back over so that the fold meets the finished edge of the patchwork. Machine-stitch around the other three sides, and turn the pillowcase right side out.

scented sachet

Packed with aromatic dried lavender, small scented sachets make ideal gifts. This is a very simple project and it is perfect for beginners, especially because it uses so little fabric. Tuck the sachets into drawers of sweaters or lingerie, or attach a ribbon loop to the top of the heart so that it can be suspended from a coat hanger to scent a closet and help keep voracious moths at bay. To replace the lavender when it eventually loses its scent, simply snip through the stitching on the hand-sewn opening.

The finished sachet measures 6 x 5½ in. ½-in. seam allowances are included throughout.

YOU WILL NEED

▶ 8-in. square of muslin for foundation fabric

▶ Scraps of silk in coordinating colors

▶ Embroidery floss

▶ Tracing paper, pencil, and pattern paper

▶ 8-in. square of linen for the back

▶ Decorative button

▶ Dried lavender

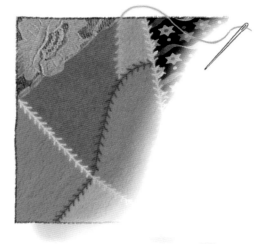

1 Following the instructions on pages 114–116, cover the foundation square with crazy patchwork silk scraps.

2 Embroider over the seams in the crazy patchwork using fly stitch. (See page 118.)

5 With right sides together, machine-stitch the front and back together, leaving a 2-in. opening.

6 Turn the heart right side out and fill it with dried lavender. Slipstitch the opening closed. (See page 116.)

3 Make a paper pattern from the template on page 122. Pin the pattern to the patchwork and cut one piece. Then pin the pattern to the linen backing fabric and cut one piece.

4 Hand-stitch a decorative button to the patchwork.

❱ handbag ❱ folder ❱ velvet bear ❱ beach bag ❱ sun hat ❱ star decorations

gifts and heirlooms

handbag

This handbag could be used during the day or added to a summer outfit for the evening. It is a handy size for a small wallet and a few make-up items. The silk fabrics give it a sophisticated feel. The colors and textures of the patchwork pieces are so subtle that I was reluctant to do much surface decoration, so I decided to add just a few mother-of-pearl buttons, which have a similar quality. Many colors and shades can be seen in mother-of-pearl, and the patchwork is like a larger-scale version in shades of emerald green. The buttons and the two ties, which become a bow, add a feminine finishing touch.

The main body of the finished bag measures approx. 6½ x 9 in.
½-in. seam allowances are included throughout.

YOU WILL NEED

- Eight 2½ x 16-in. strips of muslin for foundation fabric
- Different shades of solid-colored silks and cottons at least 2½ in. wide
- Pattern paper
- Pencil
- 18-in. square of cotton fabric for lining
- 18–22 mother-of-pearl buttons in various sizes
- 1½ x 16-in. strip of silk for handle
- 1½ x 16-in. strip of cotton fabric for handle
- 2 x 26-in. strip of bias-cut cotton for binding
- Two 1½ x 10-in. strips of cotton fabric for ties

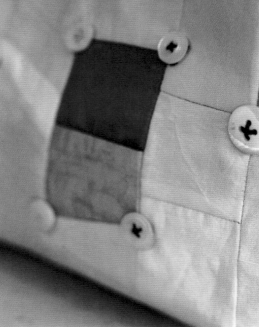

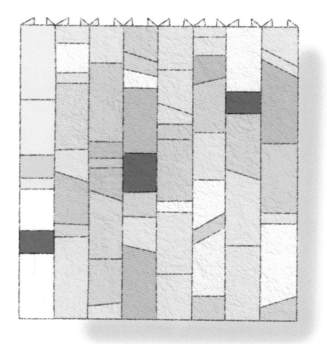

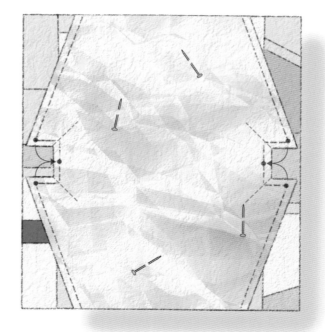

1 Following the instructions on pages 114–116, cover the eight foundation-fabric strips with crazy patchwork, keeping some of the seams parallel to the top edge and some on the diagonal. Right sides together, machine-stitch the eight strips together along the long edges. Press open the seams.

2 Using the template on page 124, make a paper pattern. Cut one piece from the patchwork and one from the lining fabric.

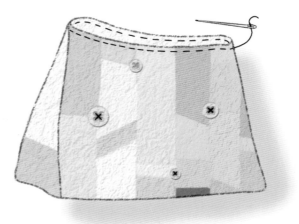

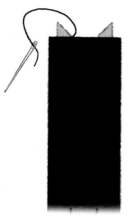

5 Wrong sides together, position the lining inside the bag. Hand-baste the lining in place along the top edge.

6 Now make the handle. Right sides together, pin and machine-stitch the strip of cotton fabric to the strip of silk, using ½ in. seams, along the two long edges. Trim the seams to ¼ in. Turn the handle right side out and press.

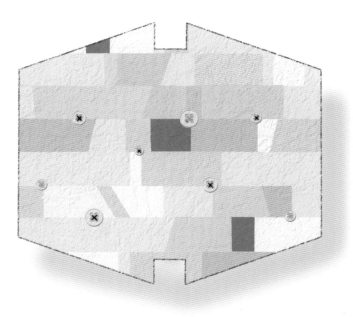

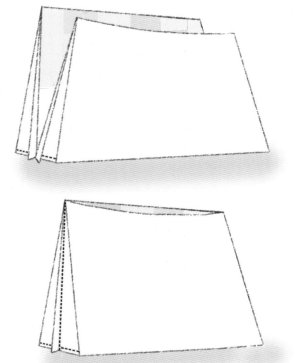

3 Sew buttons randomly over the patchwork, avoiding the edges.

4 Following the dotted lines on the pattern, fold the patchwork piece together on the inside. Following the dashed lines on the pattern, machine-stitch the base and the two sides. Repeat for the lining of the bag.

7 Make two ties. (See page 121.) Baste the ties and handle in position as shown in the diagram, with the silk side of the handle facing inward, next to the body of the bag.

8 Bind the top edge of the bag with bias binding. (See page 120.) Fold the handle and ties back to the top and slipstitch them neatly in place. (See page 116.)

folder

This folder is the perfect addition to a bookcase or desk, and a useful place to store envelopes and writing paper. In this age of e-mail communication, a handwritten letter from a friend is all the more special.

For this folder, I found a hand-embroidered piece of table linen that had become separated from a set. The floral ribbon-embroidery inspired me to use a thin ribbon rather than embroidery floss to make the arrowhead stitches that hold the pieces of crazy patchwork together. A wider ribbon, wrapped around a plain but beautiful mother-of-pearl button, is used to fasten the folder.

The finished folder measures 9½ x 14 in.

YOU WILL NEED

- Scraps of printed cotton fabric
- Two 14 x 19-in. pieces of cotton fabric
- Large-eyed needle
- Thin ribbon for embroidery
- 14 x 19-in. piece of cotton fabric for lining
- Two 2 x 8-in. strips of bias-cut silk or cotton
- Two 6½ x 7¾-in. pieces of cotton fabric for pockets
- Two 8¾ x 13-in. pieces of cardstock
- 12-in. length of wide ribbon for the tie
- 2 x 92-in. strip of bias-cut silk or cotton
- Large mother-of-pearl button

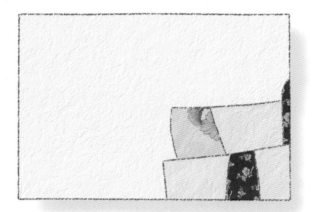

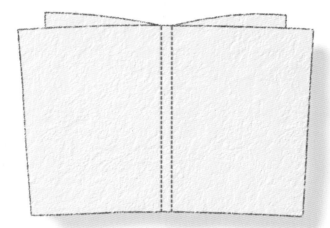

1 Cut the scraps of printed fabric into random shapes. Following the instructions on pages 114–116 and working from one side of the fabric to the other, hand-stitch them to one piece of cotton. Thread a large-eyed needle with thin ribbon and work the arrowhead stitch over the seams. (See page 117.)

2 Place the other piece of cotton on top of the lining fabric. Machine-stitch two parallel lines ½ in. apart down the center, from one long edge to the other.

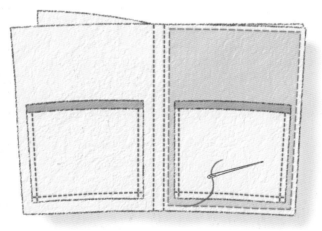

5 Place a piece of cardstock between the cotton fabric and the lining on one side of the stitched lines, positioning it as close as possible to the stitches and centering it from top to bottom. Baste around the edges to hold the cardstock in place. Repeat on the other side of the folder.

6 With the cotton sides together, baste the patchwork piece to the lining. Fold a 12-in. length of wide ribbon in half widthwise, and baste the folded edge to the center of one short side of the patchwork.

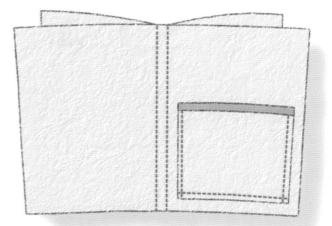

3 Using the two 2 x 8-in. strips of silk or cotton cut on the bias, bind one long edge of each pocket piece. (See page 120.) Zigzag-stitch around the remaining three sides of each pocket piece. Fold under the zigzagged edges by ½ in., and baste or press in place.

4 Fold back the cotton pieces. Pin one pocket to one side of the lining fabric 1 in. from the stitched line and 1½ in. up from the bottom. Machine-stitch around three sides of the pocket, stitching close to the edge. Attach the other pocket to the other side of the lining fabric in the same way.

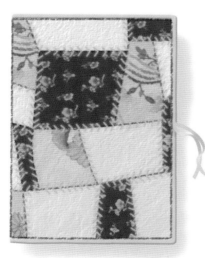

7 Bind the edges of the folder with bias-cut silk or thin cotton. (See page 120.) Stitch by hand. (You would risk breaking your machine needle if you accidentally stitched through the cardstock.) Hand-stitch a large button to the center of the other short edge of the patchwork so that the ribbons can loop around the button to hold the folder closed.

velvet bear

This endearing patchwork bear is set to become a treasured family heirloom. Make him from different textures of fabric, such as scraps of velvet and heavyweight silks, as shown here. It is important that the seams are securely stitched, as the stuffing material has to be pushed very firmly into the arms and legs to enable the bear to sit upright. Stitch his facial features in dark embroidery floss, choosing an expression to suit his character— slightly quizzical, smiling, or whatever you think is appropriate.

The finished bear is 12 in. tall.

Unless otherwise stated, stitch along the dashed lines shown on the pattern pieces on pages 125–127.

YOU WILL NEED

- 44-in. square of muslin for foundation fabric
- Scraps of at least five thin velvets and heavy silks in coordinating colors
- White and dark-colored embroidery flosses
- Pattern paper
- Polyfil stuffing
- Two buttons for the eyes
- 30-in. length of 1-in.-wide ribbon

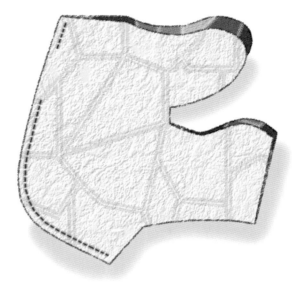

1   Following the instructions on pages 114–116, cover the foundation fabric with velvet crazy patchwork. Embroider over some of the seams using white embroidery floss and arrowhead or broken arrowhead stitch. (See page 117.)

2   Using the templates on pages 125–127, make paper pattern pieces. Pin them to the patchwork and cut out the shapes. With right sides together, pin and machine-stitch the two back pieces together down the center back, leaving an opening where shown on the pattern. Cut small notches into the seam allowance around the curves.

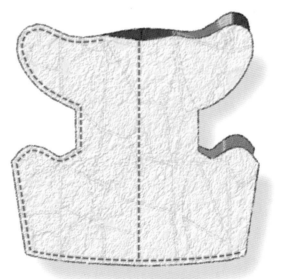

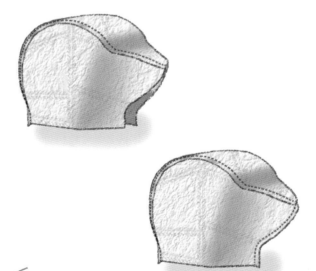

5   With right sides together, pin and machine-stitch the front to the back, leaving an opening at the top for the head and again cutting small notches into the seam allowance around the curves and at internal corners.

6   With right sides together, pin and machine-stitch one side head piece to each side of the top head piece between the tip of the nose and the back of the head. Then machine-stitch the side head pieces together between the tip of the nose and the chin. Cut small notches into the seam allowance around the curves.

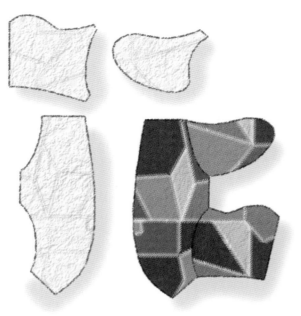

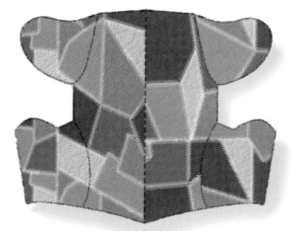

3 With right sides together, pin and machine-stitch a leg and arm piece to each front piece, again cutting small notches into the seam allowance around the curves.

4 With right sides together, pin and machine-stitch the two fronts together down the center, again cutting small notches into the seam allowance around the curves.

7 With right sides together, pin two ear pieces together along the curved edge. Starting and ending ½ in. from the straight edge, machine-stitch the two pieces together, again cutting small notches into the seam allowance around the curves. Turn right side out, fold under the raw edges, and slipstitch the straight edge by hand. Repeat with the remaining two ear pieces.

8 With right sides together, insert the head inside the body section and machine-stitch it to the body. Turn right side out. Fill the bear with stuffing. Sew the opening in the center back closed using ladder stitch. (See page 119.) Slipstitch the ears to the head. Stitch on two black buttons for the eyes and embroider the nose and mouth in satin stitch, using dark embroidery floss. Tie a ribbon around the bear's neck.

beach bag

This bag is the perfect size to hold a swimsuit and towel for a day at the beach. One of the printed fabrics I have chosen—an exotic floral print, which reminds me of Caribbean textiles—dictates the color scheme for the rest of the bag, including the lining. The embroidery picks up the two colors that form the overall color scheme—sea blue and coral red.

The finished bag measures 16 x 8 x 20 in.

½-in. seam allowances are included throughout.

YOU WILL NEED

❯ Pattern paper

❯ 1⅔ yd. muslin for the foundation fabric

❯ Printed and solid-colored cotton fabrics for the crazy patchwork

❯ Embroidery floss

❯ Tailor's chalk or dressmaking pencil

❯ 60 in. cotton fabric at least 44 in. wide for lining

❯ 9 x 17 in. piece of cotton print fabric for the base

❯ 3⅓-yd. strip of printed cotton fabric cut on the bias, 2 in. wide

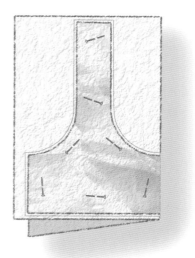

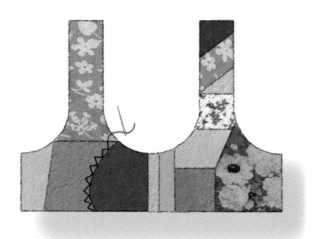

1 Using the template on page 122, make a paper pattern for the top section of the bag. Fold the foundation fabric in half, and press the fold. Pin the paper pattern to the foundation fabric, aligning the fold line on the pattern with the fold in the fabric. Cut two pieces, adding ½ in. to all edges except the folded edge.

2 Working from one side of the cotton to the other and following the instructions on pages 114–116, cover both pieces of foundation fabric with crazy patchwork, stitching curved edges by hand and straight edges by machine. Embroider over the curved, hand-stitched seams with fly stitch. (See page 118.)

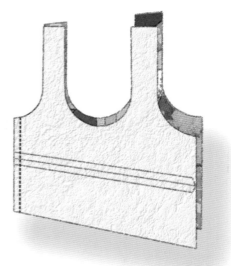

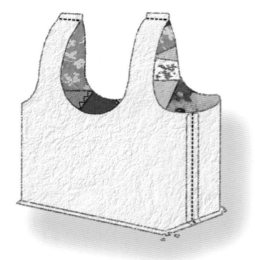

5 With right sides together, machine-stitch the two short straight sides of the bag together.

6 With right sides together, baste and then machine-stitch the bottom straight edge of the bag to the 9 x 17-in. cotton print base, making sure that the seams connecting the two sides of the bag are centered on the short edges of the base. Cut notches into the seam allowance at each corner of the bag. Machine-stitch the two short top edges of each side of the bag together to complete the handles.

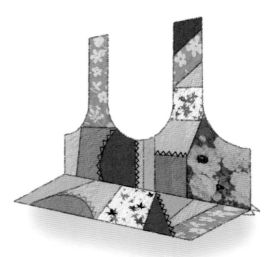

3 Cut two 9 x 25-in. rectangles from the foundation fabric. Cover the rectangles with crazy patchwork embellished with fly stitch in the same way as you did in Step 2. With right sides together, machine-stitch the long straight edge of one of the patchwork top sections to one straight edge of a patchwork rectangle. Repeat with the other top section and rectangle. Press open the seams and press each piece flat.

4 Using tailor's chalk or a dressmaking pencil, trace the shape onto lining fabric. Cut out two of these shapes, adding no seam allowance.

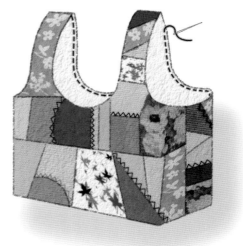

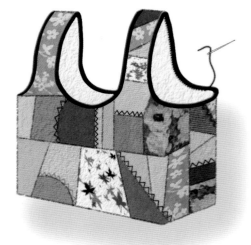

7 From the lining fabric, cut a 9 x 17-in. rectangle for the base. Repeat Steps 5 and 6 to make the lining pieces into a bag. Turn the bag right side out. Place the lining inside the bag, with its wrong side next to the wrong side of the bag. Baste the raw edges around the handles together.

8 Cover the raw edges of the bag with bias binding. (See page 120.)

sun hat

The colors that I have chosen for the crazy patchwork on this sun hat are soft and reminiscent of the 1950s. Candy-colored yellow, pink, and green are combined with eyelet, underneath which we can see a bright pink fabric that throws the pattern of the eyelet into sharp relief. The shocking pink color is further emphasized by delicate French knot stitches in the same color that are occasionally added to rows of buttonhole stitch in pink and yellow.

The sun hat provides a delicate finishing touch to a summer outfit and is practical in the bargain. You can pack it flat in a suitcase, as opposed to having to wear a straw hat on the plane when you go on vacation!

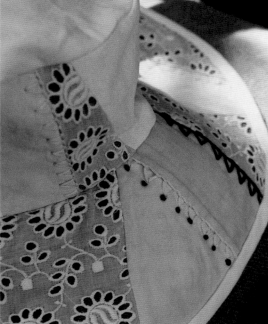

The finished hat measures approx. 15 x 6 in.
½-in. seam allowances are included throughout.

YOU WILL NEED

- Large piece of cardstock
- Pencil and string or compass
- 1 yd. of muslin for foundation fabric
- Scraps of fabric in soft colors, eyelet, and cotton fabric the same color as the lining
- Embroidery floss in two colors
- 1 yd. of lining fabric
- 23-in. square of fusible bonding web
- 2 x 55-in. length of bias-cut fabric for the brim
- 2 x 28-in. strip of lining fabric cut on the bias

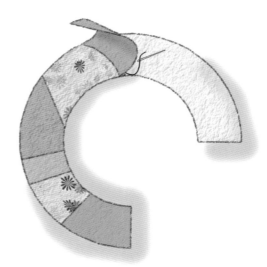

1 First make patterns from cardstock. For the brim, draw two concentric circles, 10½ in. and 22½ in. in diameter. Divide the circles into quarters. Cut out the area between the outer circle and the inner one, omitting one quarter. To make a pattern for the top of the hat, draw a circle 9½ in. in diameter. Using these two patterns, cut out one piece each from the foundation fabric, adding no seam allowance. Cut a 5 x 27-in. piece of foundation fabric for the side section.

2 Following the instructions on pages 114–116, cover the brim, top, and side pieces with crazy patchwork.

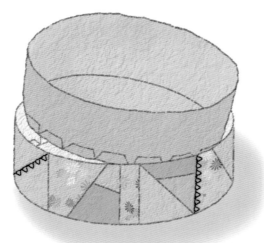

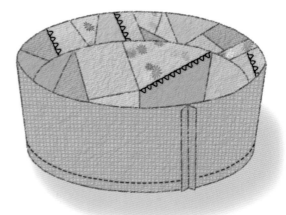

5 From the lining fabric, cut a 5 x 27-in. strip for the side of the hat and one piece using the template for the top piece. Baste and machine-stitch the two pieces together, as in Step 4. Insert the lining into the hat, wrong sides together.

6 Following the manufacturer's instructions, iron a piece of fusible bonding web to the wrong side of the patchwork brim. With right sides together, machine-stitch the two short ends of the brim together. With right sides together and aligning the raw edges, baste, and then machine-stitch the inside edge of the brim to the raw edges of the side section.

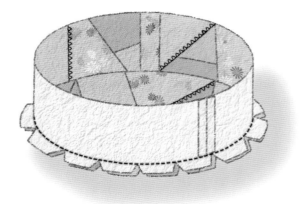

3 Embroider over some of the seams with a closed buttonhole stitch. (See page 117.) Then add French knots to some of the strips of embroidery. (See page 118.)

4 With right sides together, machine-stitch the two short ends of the side together and press this seam open. With right sides together and aligning the raw edges, baste, and then machine-stitch one long edge of the side of the hat around the circumference of the top piece, cutting small notches around the curved edge.

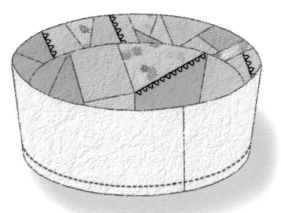

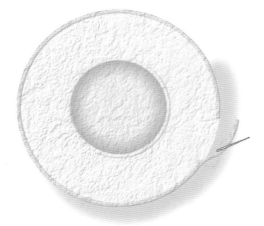

7 Using the brim template, cut one piece of lining fabric, adding no seam allowances. Machine-stitch the two short ends together. With wrong sides together and aligning the seams, machine-stitch the lining to the patchwork brim. Remove the backing paper from the fusible bonding web on the patchwork brim. Very carefully iron the two brim layers together.

8 Bind the raw edge of the brim, using the 55-in.-long bias-cut strip. (See page 120.) On the inside of the hat, cover the raw edges of the seam between the brim and side in the same way, using the length of lining fabric cut on the bias.

star decorations

These little star decorations would be perfect as Christmas tree decorations. Alternatively, you could make one very large star to crown the top of the tree. Of course, you can also use them to decorate a room year-round. Set them in between small string lights to add color and sparkle to an evening party. The colors I have chosen are not necessarily seasonal. I've taken the opportunity to use lovely printed and embroidered fabric scraps. The semi-transparent polka-dot and lace ribbons are appliquéd over a dark piece of fabric so that you can see their design more clearly. I've used them to cover some of the seams.

The finished star measures approx. 5 x 5½ in.

½-in. seam allowances are included throughout.

YOU WILL NEED

- 6½-in. square of muslin for foundation fabric
- Scraps of lightweight printed and embroidered fabrics
- Scraps of lace and semi-transparent polka-dot ribbon at least 6½ in. long
- ⅔ yd. rickrack braid
- 5½-in. square of lightweight batting
- 8-in. thin cord
- 6½-in. square of printed fabric for back of star

1 Using the template on page 123 and adding ½ in. all around, cut one star from the foundation fabric. Baste one scrap of patchwork fabric to one point of the star, and trim the edge over which you want to sew the next piece so that it's straight. Place the next piece right side down along this edge, and baste, then machine-stitch it in place. Fold the piece over to the right side, and press. Baste the remaining edges of this piece in place. Continue until you've covered the whole of the foundation fabric, then remove the basting stitches.

2 Place strips of lace and ribbon over some of the seams, and machine-stitch close to each edge to secure the strips.

5 Using the template from Step 1, but without adding a seam allowance, cut a star-shaped piece of batting. Baste the batting to the wrong side of the patchwork. It should lie within the stitching line of the rickrack braid.

6 Fold the cord in half lengthwise. Baste the loose ends to one point of the star on the right side of the patchwork, with the loose ends aligning with the raw edges of the patchwork and the loop of the cord lying within the star.

3 Trim the patchwork so that it's even with the star-shaped foundation fabric.

4 Baste a piece of rickrack braid around the edges of the patchwork, ½ in. from the edge. Machine-stitch along the center of the braid to hold it in place.

7 Using the star template and adding ½ in. all around, cut a piece of backing fabric. With right sides together, baste the backing to the patchwork. Machine-stitch the fabrics together, following the stitching line of the rickrack braid as closely as possible and leaving an opening in one side.

8 Cut small notches on the inside corners of the star and around the curves of the points. Turn the star right side out and press. Fold in the raw edges of the opening and slipstitch it closed.

techniques

TEMPLATES AND PATTERNS

Although crazy patchwork is, by its very nature, composed largely of random pieces, some of the projects in this book do require patterns or templates. The instructions for each template tell you how much it will need to be enlarged. Simply place the template on a photocopier, key in the percentage enlargement, and copy.

Cutting templates and fabric pieces

Trace the template (enlarged to the correct size) onto cardstock, template plastic, or pattern paper. Place it on a cutting mat and cut around the shape with a craft knife, exerting an even pressure. To cut straight lines, place a steel ruler or straightedge along the line, hold it firmly in place (making sure you keep your fingers safely out of the way), and run the blade of the craft knife along the edge of the ruler.

Press the fabric and lay it on a flat surface. Pin the pattern piece securely to the fabric using dressmaker's pins. If the project instructions tell you to add a seam allowance, mark it around the pattern piece on the fabric using tailor's chalk. If not, simply draw around the edge. Cut out the fabric pieces using very sharp fabric scissors.

CRAZY PATCHWORK METHODS

There are several techniques for crazy patchwork. The important thing to remember is that you almost always need to stitch your randomly shaped pieces to a larger piece of fabric, so that they are held firmly together. This is known as the foundation fabric; the best fabric to use is lightweight muslin, which is preshrunk and does not add bulk to the piece.

Stitching straight-edged pieces by machine

If your crazy patchwork consists of irregular-shaped pieces with straight edges, you can stitch them together using a sewing machine. Cover a corner of the foundation fabric with the first crazy patchwork piece and baste it in place. It doesn't matter if it overlaps the edge of the foundation piece, because it will be trimmed to size later. (Fig. 1)

1

Cut a second crazy patchwork piece, with one side the same length as one of the sides of the first piece. Place the second piece over the first, right sides together, aligning the raw edges. Baste, and then machine-stitch the pieces, stitching ½ in. from the raw edge. Fold the second piece over to the right side and press. (Fig. 2)

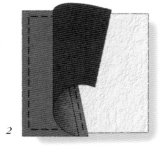

2

Baste around the remaining edges to hold the piece securely in place. Continue adding pieces in the same way until you have covered the foundation fabric.

Trim the pieces to the same size as the foundation fabric and remove all of the basting stitches. (Fig. 3)

3

Stitching short straight edges by hand

Sometimes straight edges are too short for it to be practicable to sew them by machine. If this is the case, the pieces can be hand-stitched in place using the following procedure.

Baste the first piece to one corner of the foundation fabric, in the same way as you would if you were going to machine-stitch it. (Fig. 1)

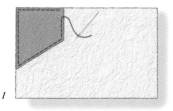

1

Press under or baste the raw edge of the next piece. (Fig. 2)

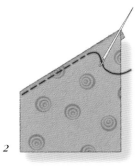

2

Position the basted edge of the second piece over the raw edge of the first piece and slipstitch it in place. Remove the basting stitches when all of the crazy patchwork pieces have been sewn down. (Fig. 3)

Stitching curved edges by hand

It is generally easier to stitch curved edges by hand, especially if you are working on a small scale. Cut small notches along the curved edge and press it under by ½ in. so that the fabric will lie flat.

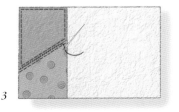

Slipstitch the edge to secure.

Stitching curved edges by machine

If your crazy patchwork pieces have long curved edges that are not very tightly curved, you can use a sewing machine to stitch them in place.

Stitching the first curved piece

Cut out your crazy patchwork shape, lay it on the foundation fabric right side up, and draw around the curve with tailor's chalk. (Fig. 1)

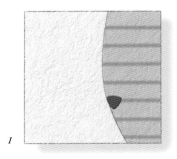

Cut small notches around the curve of the patchwork piece. (Fig. 2)

Place the patchwork piece right side down on the foundation fabric, aligning the curve with the line that you drew in tailor's chalk, but on the other side of the line. Machine-stitch along the curve ½ in. from the edge, turn the fabric back to the right side, and press. (Fig. 3)

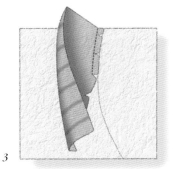

Matching a curve

Trace the curve of the first piece onto tracing paper. (Fig. 1)

Cut out the shape from the tracing paper and place it on your next piece of patchwork fabric. Draw around the curve with tailor's chalk and cut out the second patchwork piece. (Fig. 2)

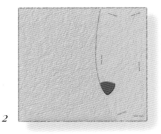

Place the second patchwork piece right side down on top of the first, aligning the curved edges, and machine-stitch ½ in. from the edge. Cut notches into the curve, making sure you do not cut into the stitching. Trim off any excess fabric. Fold the curved edge over to the right side, and press it flat. (Fig. 3)

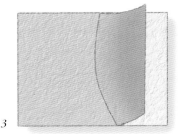

Appliquéing crazy patchwork pieces by machine

Another method is to appliqué each piece to the foundation fabric—a method that is decorative as well as functional. Lay the pieces on the foundation fabric first, to work out what edges will be visible. Fold under any edges that will lie on top when all of the pieces are fitted together. Press or baste the edges in place. (Fig. 1)

1

Pin or baste the pieces in position on the foundation fabric. Using a matching sewing thread, machine-stitch along the edges of each piece. (Fig. 2)

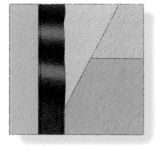

2

You could also appliqué the pieces in place by hand, using a decorative embroidery stitch such as blanket stitch (see opposite).

Using fusible bonding web

A very quick method of doing crazy patchwork is to use fusible web. It eliminates the need to turn under raw edges. (Be sure to purchase "lite" fusible web.) Following the manufacturer's instructions, iron the fusible web to the back of your patchwork fabrics.

Cut out your chosen shapes and arrange them on the foundation fabric, making sure all the edges meet as closely as possible.

When you are happy with the arrangement, remove the backing paper from each piece and iron them in place. Cover the raw edges with embroidery stitches, or appliqué ribbons, over the edges (see below).

COVERING SEAMS

Seams can be disguised either by appliquéing ribbon or lace over the top or by interspersing ribbon between pieces as the crazy patchwork is constructed.

Appliquéing ribbon or lace

One simple way of disguising seams in crazy patchwork is to cover them with pieces of ribbon or lace. Baste the ribbon or lace in place, making sure that the seams or raw edges underneath are completely covered. Machine-stitch along each edge, using a similar-colored thread.

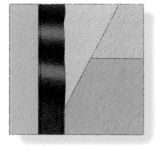

Interspersing ribbon between pieces

Baste a ribbon over one raw edge of a piece that has already been sewn to the foundation fabric. (Fig. 1)

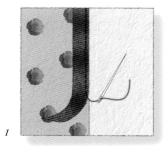

1

Place the next piece of fabric right side down on top of the ribbon, aligning the

raw edge with the edge of the ribbon and the raw edge of the first piece. Baste the piece in place. (Fig. 2)

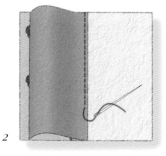

2

Machine-stitch ½ in. from the edge. Fold the fabric over to the right side, and press it in place. (Fig. 3)

3

SLIPSTITCH

Slipstitch is used to sew a folded edge almost invisibly to another folded edge or to a flat piece. Use it to secure hems, close openings in seams, and appliqué pieces to foundation fabric.

Hide the knot in the folded edge, and slide the needle through the fold and then through the lower fabric, picking up just two or three threads of the fabric at a time. Insert it into the first fold again, and continue in this way, making small, evenly spaced stitches, so that they are concealed as much as possible.

DECORATIVE EMBROIDERY STITCHES

Decorative embroidery stitches are often used to disguise where the pieces join in crazy patchwork. There are no hard-and-fast rules and the amount of embellishment is entirely up to you. Here are some stitches that you might like to try:

Arrowhead stitch

Imagine that there are three evenly spaced parallel lines marking the area of sewing. Bring the needle up through the fabric at the top of the first line and pass it back down through the fabric on the middle line at an angle of about 45 degrees. (Fig. 1)

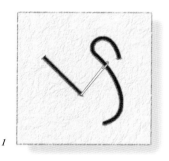

1

Bring the needle back through to the surface on the last line, level with the point at which you first brought the needle up. Take the needle back down through the point on the middle line to complete the first "arrowhead." Bring the needle out again on the first line, directly below the first point and level with the point on the middle line, and continue as before. (Fig. 2)

2

Broken arrowhead stitch

Follow the instructions for arrowhead stitch, but omit one side of each arrow on alternate sides.

Blanket stitch

Bring the thread through to the right side of the fabric, at the bottom of the area where the stitches will begin. Take the thread back through to the reverse, above and slightly to one side of the point at which you brought the needle

out. Bring the needle back through to the surface directly below the last point and loop the thread around the needle tip. Pull taut to complete the stitch.

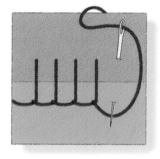

Crossed buttonhole stitch

Bring the thread through to the right side of the fabric, at the bottom of the area where the stitches will begin. Take it back down at the point that will be the top right-hand corner of the cross. (Fig. 1)

1

Bring it up at the bottom left-hand corner of the cross. (Fig. 2)

2

Take the needle back down at the top left-hand corner of the cross, keeping the thread looped. (Fig. 3)

3

Bring it up again at the bottom right-hand corner and pull it taut. (Fig. 4)

4

Closed buttonhole stitch

Bring the thread through to the right side of the fabric, at the bottom of the area where the stitches will begin. Take the needle down through the fabric, above and slightly to one side of the point at which you brought it out. This will be the top point of a triangular-shaped stitch. Bring it up through the bottom edge, next to your very first stitch, and loop the thread around the needle tip. This will be the bottom left-hand corner of the triangle. Pull the thread taut to create one side of the triangle. (Fig. 1)

1

Take the needle back down at the top of the triangle and bring it up again next to the left-hand corner, again looping the thread around the needle tip. Pull taut to form the remaining side of the triangle. (Fig. 2)

2

Cretan stitch

Imagine there are three evenly spaced parallel lines marking the area of sewing. Bring the needle up through the fabric just below the top of the left-hand line. Take the needle back through the fabric at the top of the middle line. (Fig. 1)

1

Bring the needle up again on the middle line, looping the thread around the needle tip, and pull the thread taut. (Fig. 2)

2

Take the needle back through on the right-hand line, slightly below the point on the first line, and bring it up on the middle line, slightly below the previous stitch, looping the thread around the needle tip. (Fig. 3)

3

Take the needle back through to the left-hand line slightly below the very first point and repeat the process.

Cretan stitch—open

Again, imagine that there are three evenly spaced parallel lines marking the area of sewing. Bring the needle out slightly above the bottom line and take it down on the top line. (Fig. 1)

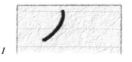

1

Bring the needle up slightly below the top line and take it down on the bottom line, crossing over the strand of thread laid down in Step 1. (Fig. 2)

2

Bring the needle up slightly above the previous point and take it down on the top line, again crossing over the strand of thread stitched down in Step 2. (Fig. 3)

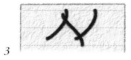

3

Couching

This is a method of fixing a continuous line of embroidery thread, cord, or ribbon on the surface of a fabric. Bring the thread up through the fabric, across the ribbon, and back down through the fabric at an angle to the ribbon.

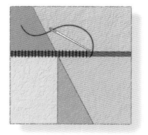

If you want to lay the ribbon down in a zigzag pattern, stitch through the ribbon at each point of the zigzag in order to hold it firmly in place

Fly stitch

Bring the needle up to the surface of the fabric, and take it back down a little further along. Bring it back up at a point midway between and slightly below the first two points, looping the thread around the needle tip, and back down immediately below the third point, so that you make a small vertical stitch that holds the loop in place.

French knot

Bring the needle up through the fabric where you want the knot to be. With the needle pointing away from you, wrap the thread twice around the needle. Twist the needle around so that the tip goes into the fabric directly beside the point where it originally emerged. Keeping the thread taut, push the needle through to the back of the fabric, pulling the thread carefully so that you make a small knot. For larger knots wrap the thread three or four times.

Cable chain stitch

Bring the needle up through the fabric and make a loop, which you hold with your finger. Take the needle down through the fabric next to the point at which it first emerged, but leave the loop loose on the surface of the fabric. Bring the needle back through to the surface below the loop.

Make a small backstitch over the loop to anchor it. Bring the needle up at the base of the "link" in the chain ready to start the next stitch. Continue in the same way to form a chain of the desired length.

Cable zigzag stitch

Each chain is made in the same way as for the cable chain stitch above, but the stitches holding them down are made at an angle to one another, so that the resulting loops form a zigzag pattern.

Daisy stitch

Bring the needle up through the fabric and take it back down at the same point, leaving a loop of thread. Hold the loop with your finger. Bring the needle up again just inside the loop and then take it back down across the loop in the thread, so that the loop is secured.

DECORATIVE STITCHES FOR JOINING PIECES

These stitches are used to join two finished edges together, with the two fabrics lying flat so that the edges meet one another.

Cretan stitch – variation

This variation on Cretan stitch can be used to join pieces of fabric together. Follow the instructions for open Cretan stitch (opposite), but work the lines horizontally rather than at an angle. Where the instructions tell you to bring the needle out on the imaginary middle line, bring it out between the two pieces of fabric.

Ladder stitch

Similar to slipstitch, but with a little more space between stitches, this is used to join two pressed edges. Bring the needle up near the edge of one piece, over where the pieces join, and down near the edge of the other piece to make a small, straight stitch. Bring the needle up again near the edge of the first piece, and repeat until the pieces have been joined.

Antique faggot hem

Working from right to left, bring the needle up on the bottom piece, slightly below the edge. Now take the needle diagonally over this edge at an angle and then underneath the top piece. Bring the needle out slightly above the edge of the top piece and then take it diagonally over this edge at an angle and under the bottom piece, so that this second stitch mirrors the first one. Continue in this way until the pieces have been joined.

BINDING

Binding is a neat way of finishing edges. You can buy it ready-made, but making your own allows you to match the binding to the other fabrics in a project.

If you are binding a curved edge, your binding must be cut "on the bias"—that is, at 45 degrees to the straight grain of the fabric—so that it will stretch enough to fit around curves.

For straight edges, the binding can be cut on the bias or on the straight grain.

Cutting binding on the bias

To mark the bias, use tailor's chalk and a drafting triangle, as illustrated, or fold the fabric diagonally so the crosswise and lengthwise grains are parallel, and press the fold. Using a ruler with tailor's chalk and scissors, or an acrylic quilter's ruler with a rotary cutter, cut out 2-in.-wide strips parallel to the first line or crease.

Joining lengths of bias binding together

Place two angled ends with right sides together along the straight grain and machine-stitch. (Fig. 1)

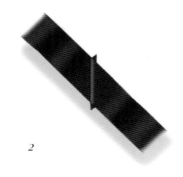

1

Press the seam open and trim away the pointed ends of the seam. Continue adding strips until you reach the desired length. (Fig. 2)

2

Binding an edge

Fold both long edges of the bias strip to the center and press. Then fold and press the strip lengthwise down the center. The fold lines will be your guidelines for stitching. (Fig. 1)

Open out the strip. With right sides together, stitch one edge of the binding to the raw edge of the right side of the piece being bound. (Fig. 2)

Turn the piece over to the wrong side. Fold the binding to the wrong side and pin it in place, with the folded edge turned under. Machine-stitch along the edge (which will be visible on the right side), or slipstitch by hand. (Fig. 3)

Binding and mitering a corner

To mark the corner position on the binding, fold the binding along the straight grain and press. Fold and press again along the opposite straight grain.

The two press marks cross in the center of the strip. (Fig. 1)

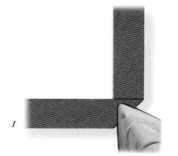

With right sides together, pin the point where the marks cross to the corner point on the piece you are binding. Following the fold line, pin the binding in place along the two edges of the piece. (Fig. 2)

Machine-stitch along the fold line to the corner, removing pins as you go. When you reach the corner, leave the needle in the fabric, lift the presser foot, and turn the work to continue stitching along the fold line. (Fig. 3)

When you have bound all of the sides of the work, turn the piece over to the wrong side. Fold the binding over to the wrong side and pin it in place along the folded edge, making sure that the corners in the binding are neatly folded. Machine-stitch (or slipstitch by

hand) along the folded edge. (Fig. 4)

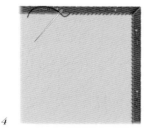

MAKING CORDED PIPING

With corded piping, a length of cord is enclosed in a strip of bias binding to create a sturdy, professional-looking finish that is particularly effective for pillows.

Making and attaching piping

Cut a strip of bias binding to the desired length. Fold it lengthwise, wrong sides together, and lay the cord inside the binding along the fold line. Pin through the fabric and the cord at one end to secure. (Fig. 1)

Fold the strip around the cord. Using a zipper foot or piping foot on the sewing machine, stitch along the edge of—but not through—the cord. (Fig. 2)

Joining lengths of piping

To join two pieces of cord together (either to make a longer piece or to join two ends of the same piece), cut the piping so that the two ends of the cord butt together. Wrap thread tightly around the ends to secure them, trimming away any excess cord to reduce the bulk.

SEAMS AND HEMS

Seams are generally finished to ensure that the raw edges do not fray.

French seam

A French seam is a very narrow seam that is used on fine or easily frayable fabrics.

With wrong sides together, align the raw edges of the two fabrics you want to join and machine-stitch ¼ in. from the edge. Trim the seam allowance to ⅛ in. and press it open. (Fig. 1)

With the seam on the inside, fold the fabric round and press it with the seamline on the outer edge. Right sides together, machine-stitch ¼ in. from this edge. Press both sides of the fabric back around so that the finished seam lies on the inside. (Fig. 2)

Double hem

This is a neat way of finishing an edge so that no raw edges are visible.

Fold under ½-in. along the raw edge of the fabric, and press or baste. (Fig. 1)

Fold the edge under again, press, and machine-stitch a line close to the first fold to secure the hem in place. (Fig. 2)

TIES

Ties provide a decorative and practical finish for all kinds of sewing projects, from pillows to seat covers.

Making ties

The fabric strips are cut in the same way as for binding (see page 119), but they can be cut either on the bias or on the straight grain. Each strip should be the required length of the tie plus ½ in., and about twice the desired final width plus 1 in. With right sides together, fold each tie in half lengthwise. (Fig. 1)

Machine-stitch along the long raw edge, about ½ in. from the edge, to make a cylinder. (Fig. 2)

Trim the seam allowance to ¼ in. Thread a darning needle with strong thread, and make a strong stitch at one end of the cylinder. Push the needle through the cylinder, pulling the end of the fabric with it, to turn the tie right side

out. Tuck in the raw edges at the ends and slipstitch the cylinder closed. Press the ties flat. (Fig. 3)

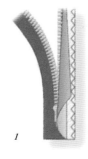

INSERTING AN INVISIBLE ZIPPER

In this method, the zipper is covered with two strips of fabric that butt together on the right side of the piece, hiding the zipper when it is closed.

Open the zipper. With right sides together, place the right-hand edge of one fabric strip on top of the zipper, aligning with the right-hand edge of the zipper fabric. Machine-stitch close to the teeth of the zipper, using a zipper foot. Repeat, sewing the left-hand side of the zipper to the left-hand side of the other strip of fabric. Zigzag-stitch along the edge of each side to secure the layers together. (Fig. 1)

Fold the fabric strips back on each side so that the folds meet in the center. Press from the right side. (Fig. 2)

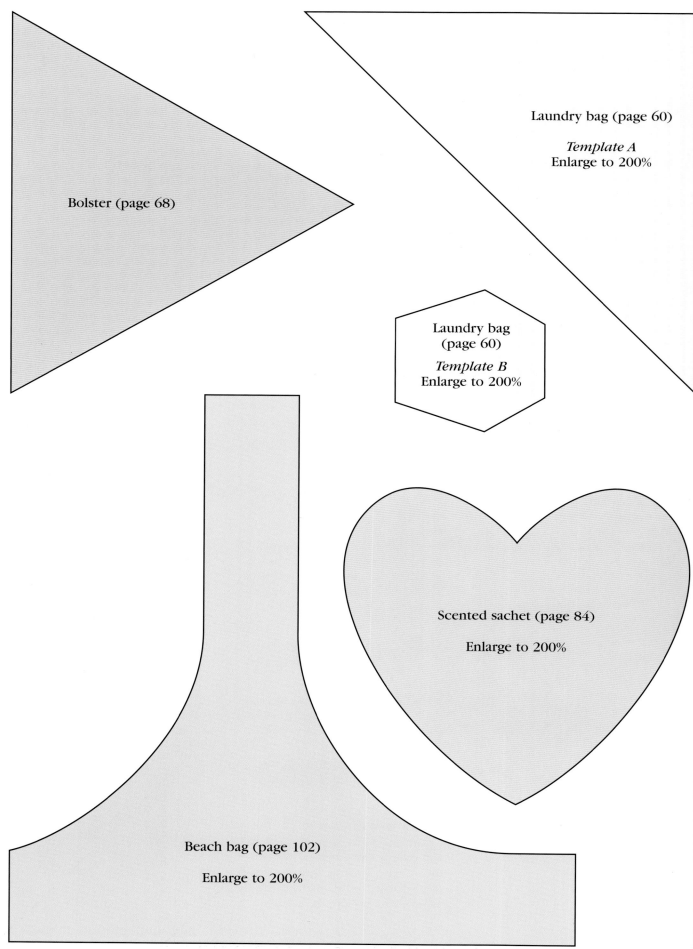

Bolster (page 68)

Laundry bag (page 60)

Template A
Enlarge to 200%

Laundry bag
(page 60)

Template B
Enlarge to 200%

Scented sachet (page 84)

Enlarge to 200%

Beach bag (page 102)

Enlarge to 200%

templates

Unless otherwise stated, templates are full size. Follow the instructions in the projects regarding seam allowances.

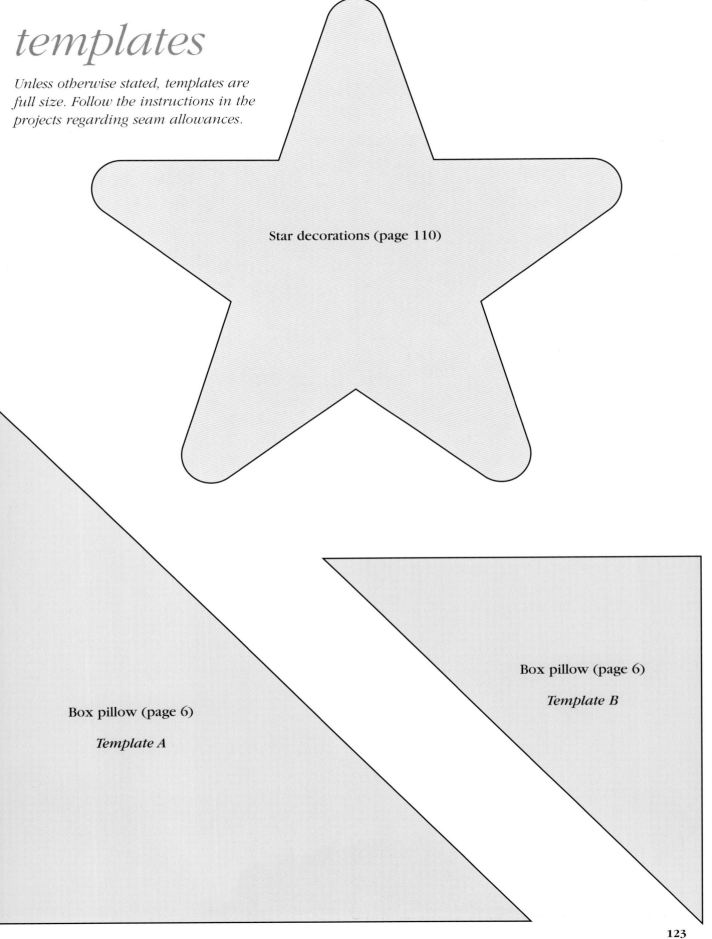

Star decorations (page 110)

Box pillow (page 6)

Template A

Box pillow (page 6)

Template B

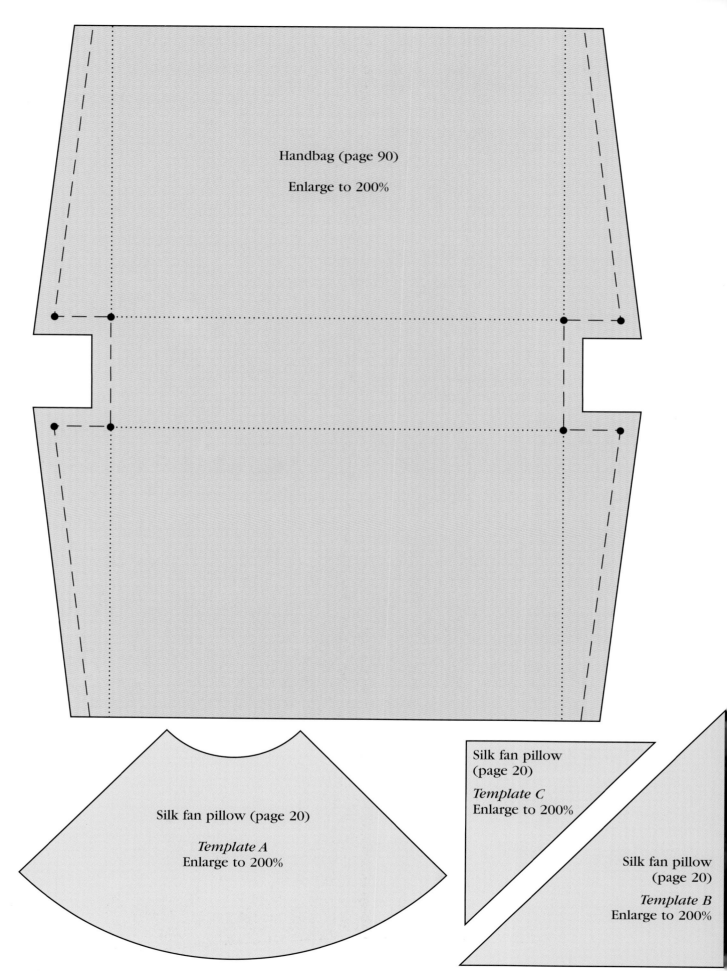

Handbag (page 90)

Enlarge to 200%

Silk fan pillow (page 20)

Template A
Enlarge to 200%

Silk fan pillow
(page 20)

Template C
Enlarge to 200%

Silk fan pillow
(page 20)

Template B
Enlarge to 200%

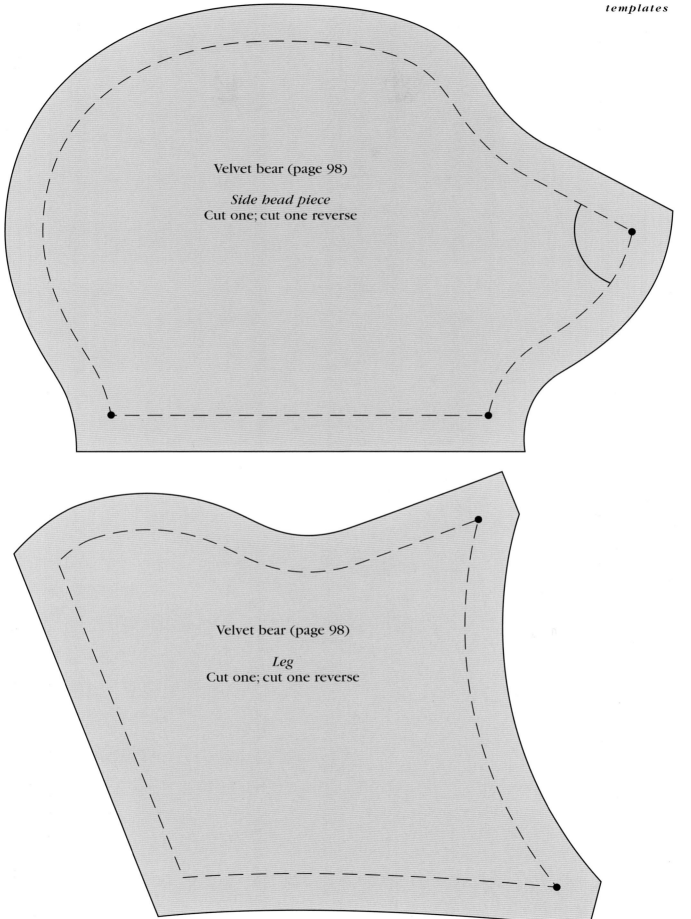

Velvet bear (page 98)

Side head piece
Cut one; cut one reverse

Velvet bear (page 98)

Leg
Cut one; cut one reverse

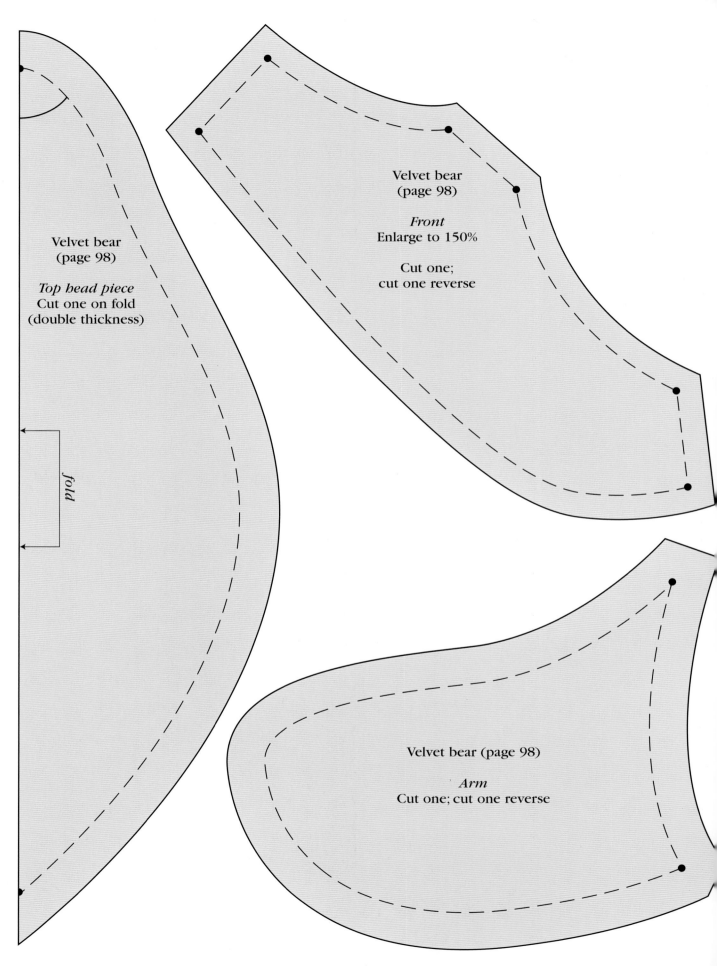

Velvet bear
(page 98)

Top head piece
Cut one on fold
(double thickness)

fold

Velvet bear
(page 98)

Front
Enlarge to 150%

Cut one;
cut one reverse

Velvet bear (page 98)

Arm
Cut one; cut one reverse

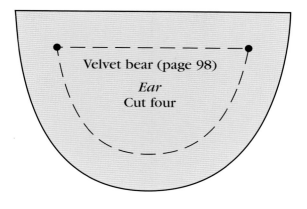

Velvet bear (page 98)

Ear
Cut four

Velvet bear (page 98)

Back
Enlarge to 150%

Cut one; cut one reverse

index

Accessories, personal
  beach bag 102–5
  folder 94–7
  handbag 90–3
  sun hat 106–9
Antique faggot hem 32, 119
Appliqué 116
  fabric pieces 116
  lace 40, 82, 116
  ribbon 41, 74, 110, 112, 116
Armchair throw 12–15
Arrowhead stitch 79, 117
  broken 117

Bags
  beach bag 102–5
  handbag 90–3
  laundry bag 60–3
Basket, tabletop 46–9
Beach bag 102–5
Beaded edging 30–3
Bear, velvet 98–101
Bedding
  blanket with crazy
    patchwork border 64–7
  quilt tied with rosettes 72–5
  pillowcase 80–3
Bedroom projects 50–87
  blanket with crazy
    patchwork border 64–7
  bolster 68–71
  cosmetics case 52–5
  dressing table runner 76–9
  jewelry box 56–9
  laundry bag 60–3
  pillowcase 80–3
  quilt tied with rosettes 72–5
  scented sachet 84–7
Bias binding 14–15, 32–3,
  119–20
Binding edges 14–15, 32–3,
  66–7, 119–20
Blanket with crazy patchwork
  border 64–7
Blanket stitch 46, 117
Bolster 68–71
Border, crazy patchwork
  for blanket 64–7
  for pillowcase 80–3
Bowl cover 30–3

Box, jewelry 56–9
Box pillow 6–11
Broken arrowhead stitch 117
Buttonhole stitch, crossed 60

Cable chain stitch 118
Case, cosmetics 52–5
Chair cover 42–5
Christmas tree ornaments, star
  110–13
Circular pattern, making 40
Circular pillow 16–19
Closed buttonhole stitch 117
Coasters 34–7
Containers
  cosmetics case 52–5
  jewelry box 56–9
  tabletop basket 46–9
Cosmetics case 52–5
Couching 67, 118
Covers
  chair 42–5
  fruit bowl 30–3
  table 38–41
  see also Pillows
Crazy patchwork techniques
  114–16
  appliquéing lace or ribbon
    40, 41, 116
Cretan stitch 15, 24, 118
  open 118
  variation 15, 119
Crossed buttonhole stitch 60,
  117

Daisy stitch 119
Decorations, star 110–13
Dressing-table runner 76–9

Edges
  binding 14–15, 32–3, 64–7,
    119–20
  covering 40, 41, 116
  joining with embroidery
    119
Embroidery, ribbon 80, 82,
  94–7
Embroidery stitches 116–19
  see also individual stitches

Faggot hem, antique 32, 119
Feather stitch 82
Fly stitch 86, 118

Folder 94–7
Foundation fabric 114
French knot 118
French seam 121
Fruit bowl cover with beaded
  edging 30–3
Fusible web 59

Gifts and heirlooms 88–113
  beach bag 102–5
  folder 94–7
  handbag 90–3
  star decorations 110–13
  sun hat 106–9
  velvet bear 98–101

Handbag 90–3
Hat, sun 106–9
Heart sachet 84–7
Heirlooms *see* Gifts and
  heirlooms
Hem, double 15, 121

Jewelry box 56–9

Kitchen projects 28–49
  chair cover 42–5
  fruit bowl cover with
    beaded edging 30–3
  placemats and coasters 34–7
  tablecloth 38
  tabletop basket 46–9

Lace, appliquéing over crazy
  patchwork 40, 82, 116
Ladder stitch 119
Lampshade 24–7
Laundry bag 60–3
Living-room projects 4–27
  armchair throw 12–15
  box pillow 6–11
  circular pillow 16–19
  lampshade 24–7
  silk fan pillow 20–3

Mitering corners
  bias binding 120
  hems 15

Ornaments, tree 110–13

Patterns *see* Templates
  circular, making 40

Pillowcase 80–3
Pillows
  bolster 68–71
  box 6–11
  circular 16–19
  silk fan 20–3
Piping, corded 19, 37, 120
Placemats and coasters 34–7

Quilt tied with rosettes 72–5

Ribbon
  appliquéing over crazy
    patchwork 41, 74, 110,
    112, 116
  couching 67
  embroidery 80, 82, 94–7
  rosettes 72, 74
Rosettes 72, 74
Ruffles 18–19, 44–5
Runner, dressing-table 76–9

Sachet, scented 84–7
Scented sachet 84–7
Seams
  French 121
  patchwork, covering 40, 41,
    116
Silk fan pillow 20–3
Slipstitch 116
Star decorations 110–13
Star-shaped embroidery stitch
  52, 54
Stitches, hand 116–19
  see also individual stitches
Sun hat 106–9

Tablecloth 38–41
Table linen
  placemats and coasters 34–7
  tablecloth 38–41
  see also Dressing-table
    runner
Tabletop basket 46–9
Teddy bear, velvet 98–101
Templates 121–7
  using 114
Throw, armchair 12–15
Ties 48–9, 121

Velvet bear 98–101

Zipper, invisible, inserting 121

CONVERSION CHART

¼ inch	6 mm
½ inch	12 mm
¾ inch	1.75 cm
1 inch	2.5 cm
2 inches	5 cm
3 inches	7.5 cm
4 inches	10 cm
6 inches	15 cm
9 inches	23 cm
12 inches	30 cm